A Fascination with Fabric

A FASCINATION WITH FABRIC
Selections from *Ireland's Own*

Eileen Casey

ARLEN
HOUSE

A FASCINATION WITH FABRIC

is published in 2014 by
ARLEN HOUSE
42 Grange Abbey Road
Baldoyle
Dublin 13
Ireland
Phone: +353 86 8207617
Email: arlenhouse@gmail.com
www.arlenhouse.blogspot.com

978–1–85132–082–0, paperback

International distribution by
SYRACUSE UNIVERSITY PRESS
621 Skytop Road, Suite 110
Syracuse, New York
USA 13244–5290
Phone: 315–443–5534/Fax: 315–443–5545
Email: supress@syr.edu
www.syracuseuniversitypress.syr.edu

Typesetting by Arlen House
Cover image: 'Woman in a Stripped Dress'
by Édouard Vuillard

CONTENTS

Social History

ACKNOWLEDGEMENTS

Thanks to the current editors of *Ireland's Own*, Phil Murphy and Sean Nolan; the editors of Women's Work, The Works, Wexford, where 'My Mother's Hands' first appeared; to John Low, editor of *Senior Times*, where 'One Fine Evening in Dalkey' was published; *InTallaght Magazine* where a version of 'Forest Bathing on La Gomera' appeared. 'In the Beginning' was shortlisted for the Fish Short Memoir Awards 2014. Thanks to Spanish Tourism, Westmoreland Street, Dublin 2; to Anne Cleary and Denis Connolly, Paris-based Irish artists and Carmel Maginn, coordinator, *The Power of Story* project.

For continuing support, grateful thanks is owed to South Dublin County Council, in particular Maria Finn, Senior Officer, Social Inclusion Unit; to Glenn Patterson, editor of 'Literary Miscellany', *The Ulster Tatler* where 'From the Royal School', was first published. 'Letter to my Daughter' was a regional winner in Age & Opportunity's Letter Writing Awards (2007). A version of 'Fine Feathers and Beauty Queens' appeared in *All Write!* (1997), an anthology compiled from the winning entries in An Post Letter Writing Awards. 'A Scarlett Moment' was shortlisted for Listowel Writers' Week Humorous Essay Prize, 2012. For help with supporting material, sincere appreciation to Silé Coleman, Local Studies, Tallaght Library, Dublin Fire Brigade, Dedalus Press, Faber & Faber, Dublin City Archives, Kieran Glennon, Valeo Foods, the Military Archives.

Gratitude and affection to Platform One Writers' Group and to Eamonn Maloney, whose publication *Tallaght: A Place with History*, proved invaluable when researching poet Alice Furlong. Sincere appreciation to The National Gallery of Art, Washington for the use of cover image, *Woman in a Striped Dress* by Édouard Vuillard.

For John

A Fascination with Fabric

Down through the years *Ireland's Own* has been a tremendous outlet for writers. This iconic publication is over a hundred years old, proof that it remains as relevant now as it was when it first appeared in print. Maeve Binchy once described the magazine as being 'like a friend', publishing experienced writers as well as first works. Indeed Maeve herself has been a great source of inspiration to writers. For this reason, I include here a memory of being invited to her home, a recollection of a lovely evening in the company of a lovely lady, first published in *Senior Times*. Because quite an amount of my poetry consists of memory poems, I also include 'From the Royal School' (*The Ulster Tatler*).

When I began to compile a selection of writings published in *Ireland's Own*, I was surprised by the number that has accumulated over the last decade or so. Most of my prose pieces are rooted in the beautiful Georgian midlands town where I grew up; Birr in County Offaly. South Dublin County features strongly also. I came to live in Tallaght as a young bride; it's been my home since the late 1970s. I'm especially pleased to include mention of Alice Furlong and Katharine Tynan, both of whom firmly established Tallaght and South Dublin on the literary map. I think these poets would be pleased by the number of well-known contemporary writers currently working in the county.

ONE CITY, ONE BOOK:

IF EVER YOU GO: A MAP OF DUBLIN IN POETRY AND SONG

> I have lived in important places, times when great
> events were decided.
>
> – Patrick Kavanagh

The objective of this award-winning Dublin City Council initiative run by Dublin City Public Libraries and Dublin UNESCO City of Literature is to encourage the reading of a book during the month of April. The selected book is connected to the capital city either by subject or by author. Dublin has shaped, and continues to do so, the imaginative lives of so many writers born here or, like Seamus Heaney and John Banville, among others, who came to live here.

One City, One Book promotes reading for enjoyment and educational purposes; encourages people to use their local libraries and book clubs and it celebrates a city which boasts one of the world's richest literary heritages. It's phenomenal to imagine that four writers associated with Dublin have been awarded the highest award for literature, becoming Nobel Laureates; William Butler Yeats (1923), George Bernard Shaw (1925), Samuel Beckett (1968) and Seamus Heaney (1995).

To date, the books selected since the initiative began in 2006 have been novels (with the exception of a short story collection, *Dubliners* by James Joyce – the 2012 choice). These works by both contemporary writers and writers who have since passed into history, reflect the broad range in literary genres abounding in the literature of the city, from Swift's satire to Stoker's gothic fantasy.

Last year's book, *Strumpet City* by James Plunkett, depicts a pivotal event in Irish social history – the mass lockout of trade unionists by employers in 1913. *The Picture of Dorian Gray* (the choice in 2010) by Oscar Wilde (which is a testimony to his aesthetic philosophy) was followed in 2011 by Joseph O'Connor's *Ghost Light*. O'Connor's novel is loosely based on the love affair between the great Irish playwright John Millington Synge and the Abbey Theatre actress Molly Allgood. Pulitzer Prize-winning author Michael Cunningham referred to *Ghost Light* as being 'A rare and wonderful book'.

Bram Stoker, born in 1847 at Marino Crescent was the 2009 choice. His enduring classic *Dracula* continues to grip the imagination of its readers in an irresistible way. Stoker was bedridden for most of his childhood and was bled repeatedly in an effort to relieve his condition. He later wrote that his long illness and the leisure it gave him provided ample opportunity for many thoughts which were to bear fruition in later years. *Dracula* continues the gothic fiction genre established by Dublin writers such as Charles Maturin and Sheridan le Fanu.

Flann O'Brien's *At Swim Two Birds* was the first novel of the city in 2006. Initially published in 1939, it is lauded as one of the funniest books ever written and not only does O'Brien poke fun at the novel form, he also emphasises its versatility. It is a novel which celebrates the power of language and the raucousness of Dublin speech. O'Brien (real name Brian O'Nolan) was born in County Tyrone. He graduated from UCD and joined the Civil Service. He is also famous for his 'Cruiskeen Lawn' column in *The Irish Times* which he wrote under the pseudonym 'Myles na Gopaleen'.

Sebastian Barry's *A Long Long Way* was the choice for 2007. Barry, born in Dublin in 1955, continues to be one of our most prestigious literary figures and as well as being a world renowned novelist, he is also a poet and playwright. Perhaps one of the most iconic books in world literature, *Gulliver's Travels* by Jonathan Swift was the book for 2008. Swift, born on 30 November 1667 in Dublin and educated at Trinity College and Oxford University, became Dean of St Patrick's Cathedral in 1713. *Gulliver's Travels* (published in 1726) is the only book for which Swift received any money.

Through the medium of prose and through writers such as Seán O'Casey, James Plunkett, Brendan Behan and Colm Tóibín, the 'voice' of Dublin and its people has reverberated throughout the world. Even though Joyce moved away from Dublin, he never truly left behind the city of his birth. If Yeats referred to the architecture of Dublin (Georgian buildings, the statue of Cú Chulainn in the GPO, the Hugh Lane Gallery and the Abbey Theatre), Joyce was more interested in the 'structures' of language itself.

Writers tend to forge their own territorial connections when it comes to place. Thomas Kinsella, for example, lived in several houses in Inchicore-Kilmainham. His father worked for Guinness and his grandfather was captain of one of the barges that ferried barrels of porter from the brewery to the 'Lady Patricia' at Butt Bridge. He attended the model school in Inchicore and then the Christian Brothers in O'Connell Street.

Austin Clarke lived in the shadow of the Black Church and knew the superstition that you could go safely round it twice but on the third attempt might meet the devil. Michael Hartnett also lived in Inchicore for a time and worked as a night telephonist in Exchequer Street. Finglas-born poet, novelist and playwright Dermot Bolger's house in Drumcondra backs onto the house where Joyce's brother Frederick died in 1884. The house featured in *Portrait of the Artist*. Although the authors chosen to date by One City, One Book have all been men, women writers such as Elizabeth Bowen (born in Herbert Place in 1889) Maeve Brennan (born in Ranelagh in 1917) and Anne Enright (winner of the Booker Prize in 2007) are, among others, very much in the canon of Irish literature.

In recognition that the city is steeped in the work of poets such as Austin Clarke, Thomas Kinsella, Paula Meehan, Brendan Kennelly, Nuala Ní Dhomhnaill, Derek Mahon, Seamus Heaney, Paul Durcan, Eavan Boland, Dermot Bolger, P.J. Daly, Iggy McGovern, Enda Wyley, Declan Collinge, among others, the One City, One Book choice for 2014 is *If Ever You Go: A Map of Dublin in Poetry and Song*. This welcome break with tradition, through a collection of poems, ballads and song, will take the reader on a virtual tour of the City of Words. Edited by Pat Boran and Gerard Smyth, themselves acclaimed poets, *If Ever You Go* is a volume of writings about Dublin, covering the period from early to modern times. It includes work by both contemporary and historical figures, among the latter, Swift, Synge, Yeats, Joyce, Kavanagh and Ó Direáin. There are songs and ballads from the city's colonial past, verses by leaders of the 1916 Rising, and portraits of the modern city with its Spire and Luas tram, its Celtic Tiger 'prosperity' and its post-Celtic Tiger challenges. I'm privileged to have two poems included in *If Ever You Go*. 'Black Ball Gown' is set in a 1970s Dublin when I lived with my sister in a bed-sit near Leonard's Corner. 'Warriors' is about a Luas tram journey I took where I celebrate the imaginative riches endowed by our new multicultural society, while still holding firmly to my midlands' roots.

The title of One City, One Book, 2014 comes from a lyric by one of our best loved poets:

If ever you go to Dublin town
In a hundred years or so
Inquire for me in Baggot Street
And what I was like to know
– 'If Ever You Go to Dublin Town', Patrick Kavanagh

More than eighty years ago, Monaghan-born Kavanagh moved to Dublin. He was as much identified with the city as with his birthplace, Inniskeen. Although he moved to London temporarily, his poetry is concerned with tensions between native rural countryside and the city. Kavanagh names the places he knew; Grafton Street and Baggot Street Bridge. He lived at 62 Pembroke Road and made famous forever Raglan Road. A seat by Baggot Street Bridge is named in his memory and serves as a response to his wish to be commemorated with 'a canal-bank seat for the passer-by'. He also mentions pubs he frequented, such as Searson's and The Waterloo. As an outsider looking in, he had a unique perspective on the city, whose canals, walkways and lanes he was familiar with. 'If Ever You Go' and 'Raglan Road' (recorded by the late Luke Kelly of the Dubliners) are two of the best known poems by a poet who lived in the city but was not quite of it.

It's somehow poignant that Kavanagh should ask to be 'inquired' about after his death, little knowing how iconic a writer he was to become. Indeed, most contemporary poets cite Kavanagh among their influences. As is the case with W.B. Yeats, Heaney always acknowledged Kavanagh, while Eavan Boland, one of our most respected living poets, cites Yeats as having a profound effect on her poetic sensibilities. Daughter of a diplomat, Frederick Boland and Frances Kelly, a post-expressionist painter, Boland was born in 1944 and enjoys an illustrious literary career. She was only 18 years old when her first collection, 23 Poems, was published. Boland introduced a whole new energy into the Irish lyric, finding poetic material in the ordinary domestic world women inhabit, writing poetry based around night-feeding and nurturing. Although she is now based at Stanford University, during a period in the 1980s she facilitated a lot of writing workshops throughout Dublin and gave readings which attracted a huge following. At that time, I was beginning to write poetry myself and so 'fired up' and with a toddler in tow, I took two buses each Friday for ten weeks, from Tallaght to Dundrum Adult Education. I found the whole experience exhilarating and certainly hugely instrumental in keeping my own aspirations alive. All of Boland's poems are memorable but 'The Black Lace Fan My Mother Gave Me', is one of my personal favourites. I met Eavan Boland again while I attended the Eastern Washington University Summer School in the Irish Writers' Centre a decade later. Again, I found her extremely encouraging and she undoubtedly remains an influential figure for a whole generation of poets.

Paula Meehan, awarded the Ireland Chair of Poetry in 2013, an honour she will hold until 2016, is also featured in *If Ever You Go*. Meehan is a poet of tremendous warmth and compassion. Like most people who are enormously gifted, she is generous with her time and her talent. She visited my writing group, Platform One (Rua Red Arts Centre) last year, an occasion that is very memorable and important in the history of our group. Born in 1955, the eldest of six children, Paula Meehan started school at St Elizabeth's in Kingston upon Thames, England, where her parents had travelled to find work. She finished her primary education at the Central Model Girls' School in Gardiner Street. Her subsequent academic career has been equally as illustrious as Boland's. Paula Meehan follows John Montague, Nuala Ní Dhomhnaill, Paul Durcan, Michael Longley and Harry Clifton in the post awarded to her by President Michael D. Higgins.

On Tour with the Jane Austen
Creative Writing Sewing Kit

> Her needlework, both plain and ornamental, was
> excellent and she might have put a sewing machine
> to shame.
> – James Edward Austen-Leigh about Jane Austen

In 2007 I put together an installation of fabric and poetry
for Birr Vintage Week & Arts Festival. The installation, in a
shop window, was a great success as it consisted of raw
silk, fans, satin gloves, regency dress and of course, poetry.
The idea for the installation came about from putting three
things together; a love of the works of Jane Austen, a set of
miniature dolls and the influence of my mother's sewing
on my imaginative life while I was growing up.

I also have to credit the effect of being surrounded by
beautiful Georgian architecture. Birr is a heritage town and
is a feast for the eye, even on the greyest day. The concept
for 'The Jane Austen Creative Writing Sewing Kit' arrived
soon after I first clapped eyes on the set of dolls.
Languishing on a shelf in a local hardware shop, they
seemed perfectly at home among the porcupine bristles of
yard brushes, tins of bright paint and miles of clothesline.
To my mind they represented characters from an Austen
novel and how those characters got on with the business of
living, no matter how dramatic turns of events became. I
placed these Lilliputians in the old sewing box I had (as a

temporary home initially). This in turn reminded me that Jane Austen lived in a period when sewing was considered to be the most appropriate activity for women. However, one of the most famous authors in the English language enjoyed both sewing and writing.

Jane Austen gathered the themes for her work from the commonplace of the domestic scenarios she experienced in her daily life. She 'sewed' from the ordinary fabric of what she saw and heard, making such wondrous 'cloths' woven with the most accurate insights into human nature. My mother completed the triumvirate of inspiration because she was a dressmaker, making the most beautiful dresses from remnants.

In 'The Jane Austen Creative Writing Sewing Kit', I wanted to highlight that cutting out a piece of fabric, following a pattern and sewing it with lines of stitching could be paralleled with plotting a novel or writing a poem. Jane Austen's needles, threads and coloured spools are living proof of her dexterity as a novelist; I describe this in one of my poems, 'Dressmaker' – (Her fingers, easy with /the fit of pen/fly across the cloth of a blank page/poetry or prose finely wrought/as a sewing-woman fluent with her needle/cuts out patterns/or sews the intricate design of a morning's gossip).

In the summer of 2008, I decided to pack all my Austen paraphernalia into two suitcases and go on tour. I felt like a travelling salesman boarding train and bus. To unsuspecting fellow travellers I was a lady of mature years setting out on a visit to a friend or family member. Little could they know that my case held swathes of pink silk and love poems. However, it has to be said that movement for a twenty-first century woman cannot compare with that of ladies in Austen's time. Women such as Mary Wollstonecraft and Maria Edgeworth certainly embarked on European tours, but these journeys were not intended to round out the educational or cultural experience of women in the same manner as men.

My intention in 'going on the road' was so the installation could be seen in libraries as opposed to a drapery shop, and in this way complete the literary end of its purpose. The 'Grand Tour' did not take place in Spain, Italy or Portugal. In my case, the 'tour' stopped off at South Dublin County Civic Library, Tallaght; Leixlip Library, County Kildare and Ennis Library, County Clare.

In all the venues, the library staff had ensured that Jane Austen's work was prominently displayed so that the novels experienced a revival for readers who maintain a regular vigil at the Austen flame and also served as an introduction to first time readers of the works. South Dublin Library introduced the 'Austen Event' with a highly-acclaimed talk by Dr Darryl Jones, Senior Lecturer at Trinity College. He made the point that we sometimes forget that *Pride and Prejudice*, for example, is a figment of the imagination, to which a wit in the audience piped up 'ah yes, but Colin Firth is very much alive and well'. Each library location provided its own space and the installation accommodated itself accordingly. Leixlip Library has a lovely gallery facility so my yards of raw silk (symbolising the raw material of imagination) looked particularly effective against pristine white walls.

Going to Ennis Library, County Clare, entailed a four hour journey and an overnight stay. I thoroughly enjoyed my visit to this medieval town. The River Fergus (complete with cheeky otters) flows through the town, bringing to mind another of the poems in the installation: 'A Journal Entry', – (A glimpse of turquoise shapes/silk of a woman/graceful as a song or birds in flight./She stretches her limbs under moonlight/pale as tulle; shades of evening scroll/memory's patterned page./She sways to a taffeta rustle, /leaves against the eaves:/longs for the season's first ball/its blizzard of dancing./ Through an open window/a river of music un-spools through a dressmaker's hands).

During the creative writing workshops, in all locations, *Pride and Prejudice* proved to be extremely popular. It's as finely tuned as a Swiss clock and inspired the participants to take up the pen. Lots of writing began in the workshops, 'lines' sewn and, using endearing characters like Mrs Bennett and Mr Collins, colourful characters drawn up. The 'interview' between Mr Collins and Elizabeth regarding his proposal gave great merriment to all, living proof that Austen's work will always endure. Romantic encounters between Elizabeth and D'Arcy brought on 'swooning' moments which were also thoroughly enjoyed.

The summer of 2008 will always be fondly remembered as the summer of Jane Austen. A younger friend remarked that going on the road with 'The Jane Austen Creative Writing Sewing Kit' was a bit like taking a rock band on tour. I think Jane herself might see the humour in this, she was always a woman far ahead of her times. Apart from anything else, new friendships have been forged and new readers brought to the work. Who knew the value of friendship more than Austen herself … 'Friendship is certainly the finest balm for the pangs of disappointed love' (*Northanger Abbey*).

ALICE FURLONG:
A TALLAGHT POET

The Furlong sisters were wild, leggy young things,
with manes of black hair, like mountain ponies, and
they were always chattering about poetry.

– Katharine Tynan

Alice Furlong was born in 1875, spending her childhood
years at Fernvale in Bohernabreena, Tallaght before the
family later moved to Bawnville House, Old Bawn. A large
part of Alice's inspiration for writing came from the world
of nature and fairy tales and no wonder. Oisín is reputed
to have returned from Tir na nÓg to Gleann na Smól in the
Dublin mountains, a landscape Alice loved so much
during her lifetime and one that remains steeped in
mythology to this day.

A staunch Catholic, Alice's poems enabled her to praise
God through her verse and express her gratitude for the
many wonders offered by each changing season. Local
rivers, such as 'The Dargle' and 'The Dodder' feature
prominently. Until the age of fourteen she was well known
in the area as a gifted singer, a talent that was actively
encouraged by her mother, a native Dubliner. As a young
girl, Alice made regular trips to the Royal Irish Academy.
The eventual losing of her sweet voice caused Alice to later
remark, 'I do not know what happened but my voice took
wings and flew'. Luckily, her 'voice' soon found a new
outlet through poetry.

Although Katharine Tynan, living at the time in Kingswood and to whom William Butler Yeats was a regular visitor, was a contemporary poet in South Dublin, Alice Furlong cut her own literary swathe. Her debut collection *Roses and Rue* (1900) was published to critical acclaim by London publisher Elkin Mathews. This particular collection also brought recognition as far afield as America where Alice's work is still admired today. Right from the beginning her exceptional ability with words was evident. When she first began writing her verse, her poems were accepted immediately by the then popular literary magazine, *The Irish Monthly*.

A dark beauty, Alice was one of four girls, the family's literary life resembling the Haworth Brontés in many respects in that, as well as being avid readers, all but one of the sisters wrote. Curiously however, Alice is the only Furlong to declare herself an author on the 1911 Census. However, the sisters were uniquely united by their common interest in nursing. All of them trained at Dr Steevens' Hospital, Dublin.

Alice's father, James Furlong, was a well-known enterprising individual, originally from Wexford. A sports journalist with *The Irish Independent* newspaper in a time when television and radio broadcasts did not exist, his colourful turn of phrase and ability to enthral his readership, ensured he was always working. He was also heavily connected with the breeding and training of winning greyhounds and horses.

Alice was a fluent Gaelic speaker and a member of Inghinidhe na hÉireann (Daughters of Ireland). When Queen Victoria visited Dublin in 1900, one of the planned events to encourage Dubliners to turn out was a Children's Picnic Party which took place at the Phoenix Park. Alice was instrumental in organising a highly successful alternative picnic (the Patriotic Children's Treat) which was held on 1 July 1900 in protest at Victoria's visit. She was also a friend of James Connolly and was involved with the 1913 Lockout, often cycling from Tallaght to Liberty Hall. Among the literary circles she mixed in at the time were Lady Wilde and Fanny Parnell, sister of Charles Stewart Parnell.

Despite her success as a poet, Alice was no stranger to tragedy. Her father James died at the young age of forty-two having sustained a fatal injury at the racetrack. He was brought to Dr Steevens' Hospital where Alice herself happened to be on duty. Alice's sister Katherine had already died, at the age of twenty-two, from consumption not long before this tragedy. Eleven weeks after the death of James Furlong, Alice's mother passed away, probably from a broken heart. Unhappiness also manifested itself for Alice when the family moved out of Tallaght for a time to live in Glasnevin. The depth of feeling wrought by this event is expressed in one of her most famous verses 'In Exile', which reflects a sense of deep alienation when not living in the little village under the Dublin mountains – (There is a little house by Tallaght town,/None may deny me,/When the sun is set, and the crescent moon gone down,/Thither I'll hie me;/I shall find welcome there,/and never a frown – /Or my dreams belie me!) Kathleen O'Brennan, a journalist and friend of Alice wrote of her that, 'Her love of the Irish language was only shared with her love of Tallaght'.

After the leaders of the 1916 Rising were executed, Alice faded out of public life. She personally knew a lot of the men who lost their lives, including Padraic Pearse, and was affected enough by the outcome of the Rising to never again write in English. Alice died at the age of seventy one and is buried in Tallaght Cemetery which was her express wish. Other works by Alice Furlong include *Tales of Fairy*

Folk and *Queens and Heroes*. She is also credited with the first translation of Shakespeare's *Macbeth* into Irish.

CHARLOTTE'S WAY

I am no bird; and no net ensnares me: I am a free
human being with an independent will.

    – Charlotte Brontë, *Jane Eyre*

On 29 June 1854, Charlotte Brontë and Reverend Arthur
Bell Nicholls, her father's curate, were married at Haworth
Church in West Yorkshire. The newlyweds left by train for
North Wales, crossing from Holyhead to Dublin, and from
there to Banagher, County Offaly, to honeymoon at Cuba
Court. The town's Shannon fortifications were updated
and strengthened because of the French invasion scare.
Banagher was still a garrison town when Brontë arrived,
and remained so until 1863. Also in existence then was The
Royal School, established in 1628 under the provisions of a
charter obtained by Sir John Mac Coghlan from Charles 1.
It moved to Cuba Court in 1818 but would close in 1890.

Anthony Trollope had been a post office clerk in the
town in 1841 and wrote his first two novels during his
stay. As well as having his creative imagination awakened
in Banagher, Trollope is credited with inventing the letter-
box. Like Trollope, Bell Nicholls had also spent time in
Banagher, County Offaly. Much of his childhood and
youth were enjoyed at Cuba Court at the Royal School
which came under the headmastership of his uncle
Reverend Alan Bell some time later. While staying at Cuba
Court, Charlotte made many visits to the rectory at Hill

House, perched regally on a hill overlooking the town and the residence for the incumbent minister to the nearby Church of Ireland chapel of St Paul's.

Over a century later, also in the month of June, I'm attending a talk on endangered species, in particular the corncrake, by Bird Watch Ireland in Crank House, on Main Street, Banagher. Crank House is a beautiful seventeenth century bow-shaped Georgian building, now used as a Bord Failte approved hostel and as a base for organisations such as Bird Watch Ireland.

I walked the few hundred yards from the outskirts of the town to the venue, down Banagher's steep hill. It's a small distance when the 6,000 odd miles or so the corncrake flies to get here is taken into account. Twelve thousand miles in total for the round trip to Africa. I thought about Charlotte Brontë and her new husband walking the very same street in the same month. How her skirts might have swept along the well-trodden path, her small feet hurrying to match the long stride of her husband. I wondered if they had visited the nearby Callows, home not only to the corncrake but also to lapwing (plover), snipe and redshank. Charlotte's romantic nature would undoubtedly have been drawn to the beauty of the natural world in Banagher, a town that sits on the banks of the River Shannon. The Callows surrounding the Shannon are hay meadows thick with iris, cow parsley, a glorious habitat for birds. The corncrake, which is roughly the same size as the mistle thrush, likes to hide in long grasses and is seldom seen in daylight hours. Instead, the crex crex call can be heard most plainly at night. I imagine Charlotte, dressed perhaps in a simple white muslin gown, wearing a sensible shawl around her shoulders and wearing sturdy shoes, inclining her head on her husband's shoulder and listening out for the distinctive sound. At the top of Keeraun Hill, just in the centre of Banagher, she may have looked down towards Galway.

Hill House in Banagher is now a well-known guest-house called Charlotte's Way, in recognition of the famous author who went there on her honeymoon. It is the only Irish house to have associations with the Brontés. Over the years it has been visited by members of the world-renowned Bronté Society. The imposing steeple of St Paul's church nearby strikes a gothic note against the skyline. The steeple of St Rynagh's Catholic Church wasn't added until 1872. Hill House still retains the original layout and some original features, including a pen drawing of the house as it was in Charlotte's time, complete with stables and tennis court. The house very much retains the atmosphere of a rectory, calm, dignified and elegant in a gracious way. It has a lovely 'library' air about it.

I could well imagine Charlotte in the study, relaxing quietly with Arthur, laying aside her book before idly glancing out the window. Her gaze would travel past the vast expanse of parkland which is now replaced by a roadway, her colourful imagination stoking up new characters in exciting scenarios. Perhaps, struck by the architectural drama of the Napoleonic martello tower beside the Shannon, her thoughts again strayed to her most famous creation, Jane Eyre and to Bertha Mason, Rochester's violently mad wife who haunted the upper floors of Thornfield Hall.

Then, with the lamp burning bright on the lace covered table beside the bookcase, conversation may have turned to the possibility of a trip to the nearby Slieve Bloom mountains. After all, Charlotte spent most of her life walking on the Yorkshire Moors, a wild setting which filters through her passionate evocation of both character and place in *Jane Eyre*. The weather during the midlands summer was more than likely clement for her visit, unlike the winter of 1880 which has gone on record for the terrible frost that lasted seven weeks, during which the Shannon was frozen and locals were able to cross it with carts of hay.

Alas, Charlotte Brontë died at Haworth in 1855. Who knows what may have transferred from her visit to Banagher into her work? Her lyrical imagination must surely have been fired by the gothic atmosphere of a midlands town at dusk, the spire of St Paul's rising majestically. Shortly after Charlotte's death, Arthur Bell Nicholls returned to Banagher and settled in Hill House with his aunt Harriett Bell and her daughter Mary Anna. Arthur and Mary Anna, his cousin, were married in 1864. Arthur died in 1906 aged 87 and Mary Anna died in 1915, aged 85. Both are buried in the graveyard of St Paul's Church.

SEAMUS HEANEY (1939–2013)

I can't think of a case where poems changed the world, but what they do is they change people's understanding of what's going on in the world.

– Seamus Heaney

The recent death of Seamus Heaney, revered in his lifetime both nationally and globally, marks a sad, untimely passing. As well as being a renowned academic and poet, Seamus Heaney was a man with many other sides to his personality. Father, husband, brother, scholar, poet, humanitarian, statesman, the list goes on. In all the generous eulogies that have been recorded after his death however, friend and compassionate human being are traits that continually emerge.

Indeed, one incidence of such warmth easily comes to mind. At Listowel Writers' Week in 2008, a Lisburn friend of mine, who had won a prize at the festival, was hoping to have a photograph taken with this giant of letters as he too was in attendance. He very graciously consented to her request, making the occasion very special for her. At his funeral mass on 2 September 2013 at the Sacred Heart Church in Donnybrook, Dublin, Chief Celebrant Monsignor Brendan Devlin made the telling remark regarding the poet's ability to communicate freely with people from all walks of life: 'He could just as easily speak to the King of Sweden, an Oxford Don or an old neighbour from south Derry'.

It is this ability to cross language registers and forge connections in surprising places that epitomised Heaney's writing from the very beginning. Born on a fifty acre farm in County Derry (Mossbawn), Heaney's father Patrick represented rural tradition while his mother had roots in industrialisation. Her people were in service and also worked in the local linen mills. A further tension in the household, which again informed the poetry, was due to the loquacious nature of Heaney's mother, Margaret Kathleen McCann, as opposed to the silent figure his father generally posed. This childhood on a small farm was to bear literary fruit in abundance. Throughout his illustrious life of letters, Heaney returned again and again to these roots, his memories never failing to surprise and startle him with new insights at every stage of his creative development. He was widely considered Ireland's greatest poet since William Butler Yeats but Heaney himself also spoke of being influenced by Robert Frost, Gerard Manley Hopkins and, of course, Patrick Kavanagh, among others.

The eldest of nine children, Heaney's rural roots were to prove the bedrock of his literary sensibilities. His poems about childhood have the sharp edge of an enquiring and multi-faceted imagination while also containing sensitivity and a great deal of tenderness. Memory poems about his mother are among his finest. One particular sonnet comes to mind (From 'Clearances 5'), 'In Memoriam M.K.H., 1911–1984', he talks about folding sheets with his mother, determining their differences and their acceptances in lines: 'In moves where I was x and she was 0/Inscribed in sheets she'd sewn from ripped-out flour sacks.'

A personal memory of my own is of going to Dundalk Town Hall about ten years ago. We drove up from Dublin, a small party of three very happy people knowing we were in for pure listening pleasure. We weren't disappointed. When we arrived, we could scarcely find parking so packed was the town as a result of the poet's appearance. He had 'rock star' audience rating and for a poet that was certainly unusual. The one thing I remember most of all from that night was the rapt expressions on the faces of the audience, a great sense of wanting to hang on every single word. Heaney himself was in fine form, tempering his reading with light-hearted asides. He took us on a journey that has remained in our consciousness and awakened us to the possibilities of what true greatness can produce. It was also a very life-affirming evening. His smile came readily, the trademark creasing of his rugged features, the eyes disappearing into mirth.

Faber & Faber have published Heaney over a period of almost five decades. In 1966, Heaney's collection *Death of a Naturalist* appeared to critical acclaim. It won several literary awards including the Cholmondeley Award and the Gregory Award. One of the more famous, and often quoted poems from this collection, 'Digging', signals Heaney's intention from early on to make his way in life through writing: 'Between my finger and my thumb/The squat pen rests; snug as a gun.' Heaney's father chose farming but his son decided to 'dig' with his pen in the rich soil of the imagination, a soil that never failed him over his glittering life as a writer of great literature. So monumental was his talent that in 1995 Heaney received his greatest critical validation when he was awarded the Nobel Prize in Literature 'for works of lyrical beauty and ethical depth, which exalt everyday miracles and the living past.' *Death of a Naturalist* also includes a well-known poignant poem which often features on the Leaving Certificate Curriculum, 'Mid-Term Break'. This poem recounts Heaney coming home from boarding school in 1953 to attend the funeral of his four-year-old brother Christopher who was killed in a road accident. This poem is simple yet devastating. It shows clear empathy with the human condition, the reactions of others in a grief-stricken household while all the while holding onto his own keen observational prism. The description of the child's coffin as measuring 'a foot for every year' is a heartbreaking image. It is fitting somehow that Heaney is now buried with Christopher in Ballaghy Cemetery, County Derry.

To return again to Monsignor Devlin's assertion regarding Heaney making himself available to people from all walks of life, poets all over the world will know the truth of this. Poets like myself who have been fortunate over the years to open an anthology and find work by Seamus Heaney alongside our own. In my case, the first time this happened was in 1988 in a publication entitled *Poets Aloud Abu* (Ink Sculptors Press, Cork). This anthology, edited by Patricia Scanlan, also included names such as Mary O'Donnell, Leland Bardwell, Pat Boran, Marie Bradshaw (Bradshaw Books) and a host of others. Some of the purchase price was donated to give severely physically-handicapped writer Davoren Hanna (13 at the time; he died in 1994), more ease in life. A more current publication where Heaney once more showed his generosity to other poets, myself included, came as recently as 2013 in a publication by Revival Press, honouring another wonderful Irish poet, Michael Hartnett, *I Live in Michael Hartnett*, (edited by James Lawlor). One of my biggest joys in this regard however, was in December 2007, opening *Poetry Ireland Review* (Issue 92, edited by Eiléan Ní Chuilleanáin) and seeing my poetry in public places exhibition ('Reading Fire, Writing Flame') alongside Heaney's collaboration with artist Barrie Cooke. It is now a treasured keepsake.

Each of us will have our own particular favourite poem. I cannot ever go to Clonmacnoise (a favourite excursion) without remembering Heaney's poem 'Lightenings viii' (from *Seeing Things*, 1991). For me, it shows how a poet, as indeed ourselves as human beings, must be constantly surprised by life, its events, its unexpectedness. In the poem the monks of Clonmacnoise are at prayer when a ship appears above them. The anchor hooks itself onto the altar rails and then a crewman shins down the rope and struggles to release it. But he doesn't succeed so the Abbot says: 'This man can't bear our life here and will drown.' Eventually, the Abbot and the monks help the man free the ship and the man climbs back: 'Out of the marvellous as he had known it.' This poem reminds us that the act of being startled by life lies in jolts of recognition, being able to see the extraordinary in the ordinary.

There remain countless stories of Heaney's generosity to younger, upcoming poets. Fellow Northern Ireland writer and Pulitzer Prize winning poet Paul Muldoon was mentored by Heaney and he remembers him with great eloquence. Muldoon says that one of Heaney's strengths as a human being was his capacity to gather us all up in his arms, to keep us safe as it were. Other testimonies lie in the numerous letters sent to Heaney replied to by his own hand. There are many lasting memorials to this life-affirming poet, a poet who in the words of former Poetry Ireland Director Theo Dorgan, 'squared up to his gift' and 'didn't let it crush him, as it crushed so many'. The Seamus Heaney Centre for Poetry at Queen's University, Belfast, opened in 2004, is one such memorial.

Seamus Heaney had that rare gift of performing balancing acts. This meant that while he was first and foremost a husband and provider to his wife Marie and their three children, Michael, Christopher and Catherine Ann, he could still hold down professorships in two continents, all the while writing poetry that will continue to be read long into the future. The man is gone alas but the poetry lives on.

JOHN HEWITT AND THE GLENS OF ANTRIM

I fear their creed as we have always feared
The lifted hand against unfettered thought
                                    – John Hewitt ('The Glens')

Over forty years ago when I named my first rubber doll I had good reason to christen her Mary Ann. My mother's favourite song at that time was 'At the Ould Lammas Fair in Ballycastle Long Ago', sung by Ruby Murray and composed by John Henry 'The Carver' McAuley. The songwriter was a sculptor of bog oak and also a proprietor of a bog oak shop in Ann Street, Ballycastle. Unfortunately he died in 1937 before his song became famous.

The oldest fair in Ireland, the Lammas Fair has been continuing uninterrupted for three centuries, taking place in August each year to celebrate the festival of Lughnasadh. Snatches of McAuley's song often come back to me, the most recurring line, 'Did you treat your Mary Ann to some dulce and yellow man', is one forever embedded in memory, together with my mother's sweet voice filling the house while she baked bread or washed clothes on the wooden washboard. It was much later before I discovered that 'dulce' was seaweed and 'yellow man' a honeycomb treat.

Ballycastle itself is a village overlooked by Knocklayde Mountain, a mountain flanked by two of the nine Glens of Antrim, Glentaisie (named after Taisie, the blond-haired

Princess of Rathlin Island that legend reports as having dazzling blue eyes) and Glenshesk (Glen of the Sedges). Rathlin Island is also the birthplace of one of our own most famous singers, Mary Black. There are nine glens in total, the other seven, named for their individual characteristics, are: Glen of the Arm, Ploughman's Glen, Edwardstown Glen, Glen of the Rush Lights, Glen of the Slaughter, Brown Glen, Glen of the Plough. Before efficient transport made access so much easier, the physical isolation of the glens gave them a mysterious and elemental beauty which sparked a lot of poetry, tales and myths. Rivers bisected the land from west to east and the track from Cushendun to Ballycastle crossed Loughareema, 'the vanishing lake'. One day it was empty, the next full. It is said that horses often brought passengers to their watery graves.

The Glens of Antrim have proved to be a source of inspiration for Northern poet John Harold Hewitt (1907–1987). Hewitt was the first significant poet to emerge in the 1960s before the rise of notables such as Seamus Heaney, Derek Mahon and Michael Longley. A socialist and romantic, his poetry collections are *The Day of the Corncrake* and *Out of My Time: Poems 1969–1974*. Hewitt's work was influenced by W.B. Yeats, William Morris and William Blake. It's not difficult to imagine why these literary giants had such an effect on Hewitt. Yeats, with an interest in mysticism and mythology, evoked for Hewitt the spiritual nature of landscape while Blake, rooted in the urban, represented the realities of society when viewed through the prism of the city. Craftsman, socialist and poet, William Morris's *News from Nowhere*, imagines a pastoral, free from nineteenth-century industrial pollution.

Although Belfast born, landscapes which are evoked most frequently in Hewitt's verse are the Glens of Antrim and he wrote many evocative poems about them and their people. Hewitt had no doubt that each glen was unique in its own way and in a poem, 'The Glen of Light', he wrote: 'This open glen's so brimmed with air and light/That space itself has body, palpable'. Written specifically about the brown glen, Hewitt's poem 'Glendun on a Wet Day' extols the healing, nurturing and energetic properties of water: 'The sounds of running water are its own; Its nature's patient, pliant to all use'.

Glendun is a place of much story and imaginative possibility. It is the site of the architecturally-splendid Charles Lanyan Viaduct Bridge. The stone for the bridge was quarried in the townland of Layde and brought to Cushendun Harbour by boat. The rest of the journey to the construction site was completed by horse and cart. Further along in Cregegh Cemetery is the Fuldiew Stone and its sad story of lost love. Of Glenariffe Hewitt composed the words: 'The raw earth gashed with water cups the sky,/with grey clouds moulded cold and desolate'. Glenariffe, meaning Glen of the Plough, presents perhaps a harsher image of nature and its elements. Known also as the Queen of the Glen, Glenariffe comprises a valley of ladder farms and caves which were inhabited until the 1800s. U-shaped Glenariffe is the result of a combination of volcanic activity and glaciations.

To celebrate the work and ideals of John Hewitt, the society which bears his name was founded in 1987. The John Hewitt Society, based at the Market Place Theatre & Arts Centre, Armagh, organise events throughout the year which includes the only literary and scenic tour of the famous Glens of Antrim. Every July, the John Hewitt International Summer School takes place which provides a week of lectures, workshops, readings and theatre themed around the work of John Hewitt. Also on offer are art exhibitions. The Summer School offers scholarships to students who wish to attend, a worthy enterprise indeed.

MEETING WILLIAM TREVOR, MASTER CRAFTSMAN

> There is an element of autobiography in all fiction in
> that pain or distress, or pleasure, is based on the
> author's own. But in my case that's as far as it goes.
> – William Trevor

Being part of the excitement surrounding the
announcement of what is now an Irish literary institution,
the IMPAC shortlist, is an experience I'll always savour.
The IMPAC Literary Award is an initiative of and
administered by Dublin City Council and is a partnership
between the Council, which is the municipal government
of Dublin and IMPAC, a product improvement company
which operates in over 50 countries. The award is the
longest and most international of its kind and involves
nominations from libraries from all corners of the globe
and is open to writings in any language.

Before the 2011 event it was made known that there
were three Irish writers on the shortlist and that one of
them would be in attendance. As it turned out the three
writers are internationally famous; William Trevor (*Love
and Summer*), Colm Toibín (*Brooklyn*) and Colum McCann
(*Let The Great World Spin*). In attendance at the event were
the Lord Mayor, Gerry Breen, Jane Alger (Dublin
UNESCO City of Literature), the Australian Ambassador
Bruce Davis, Margaret Hayes, Dublin City Librarian and
the Honourable Loyola Hearn, the Canadian Ambassador,

among others. Then lo and behold! Across the room was none other than William Trevor, a writer of such towering genius and sensitivity.

As I looked at him I couldn't help thinking about one of his most memorable works, 'The Ballroom of Romance', set in the 1950s, and filmed with Brenda Fricker and John Kavanagh, two wonderful actors who brought the repressive atmosphere of an Ireland in recession to life. The air of melancholy landscape that Trevor captures so well is remarkable. Indeed, it is said of Trevor that he is the most astute observer of the human condition currently writing in fiction. That whole era of showband mania, hair lacquer, stiletto heels and shorter hemlines/puffed out skirts came alive for me again. As the youngest of six children and having three older sisters, I grew up with the music of Eileen Reid and The Cadets and my sisters jiving to The Dixies in our cramped bedroom. There was also that great sense of young women growing up, in search of romance in our local dancehall, the Marian Hall.

Now here he was in the same room, a quiet, unassuming man of mature years (he was born in 1928), deservedly shortlisted for *Love and Summer*. Trevor's fourteenth novel, although barely 200 pages in length, is made rich by his long practised arts.

Although he has written hundreds of short stories (for which he is best known), novels and plays, William Trevor still has tremendous passion for the written word and writes every day (when he's not at the announcements of shortlists or similar). Writing every day (his preference is for blue paper) is important to him and especially in the early morning, the best time of the day. Writing since early childhood, William Trevor remembers as a young boy in school being given regular exercises to write, six lines long, on themes such as 'A Rainy Day'. He found these exercises very 'challenging' but a great apprenticeship in precision.

Chiselling away redundant wordage is second nature to him as he started out initially as a sculptor, working in that medium until the age of thirty when he realised 'I preferred to work with people, there's very little story in abstract art'. At the age of thirty-six he went on to win the prestigious Hawthorden Prize for Literature and since then he is no stranger to literary fame, winning the Whitbread Prize three times and being nominated five times for the Booker Prize. Living in Britain these past years, he's also been knighted by a recent visitor to our shores, Queen Elizabeth II, for his services to literature.

Although he is now in his eighty-third year, William Trevor still retains his astute observational faculties and claims to have 'a beady eye' for a story. This certainly served him well back in 1972 when he was driving by the Rainbow Ballroom of Romance in the village of Glenfarne, County Leitrim and saw this name written on a sign. From such small details great works are born. We should be very grateful to Glenfarne's ballroom built in 1952 and modernised in 1959 when rural electrification reached it and also the laying down of water pipes.

Responsible for over two hundred and fifty marriages, the Rainbow Ballroom of Romance in Glenfarne is currently undergoing a renaissance. Fundraising events are ongoing in order to refurbish the ballroom and convert it into a museum of showband memorabilia, a tourism information centre and fully-functional community centre.

'The Rainbow in Glenfarne', is the title track from a CD specially compiled as a fundraising venture to include old favourites from the showband era, Big Tom, Mick Flavin, Jimmy Buckley and Philomena Begley.

We can thank William Trevor for immortalising the ballroom in writing 'The Ballroom of Romance' which helped to put Glenfarne on the map, generating interest in its history throughout the world.

POETS AT THE WHITE HOUSE, LIMERICK

To have great poets, there must be great audiences
too.

– Walt Whitman

Since it first offered a platform for both established and
emerging poets in 2002, the White House Poets is now
very much part of the literary landscape in Limerick and
abroad. Poets from as far afield as the US and Australia
have featured with homegrown notables such as Knute
Skinner, John Liddy, Ciaran O'Driscoll, Paddy Bushe and
Desmond O'Grady. I was very fortunate to recently add
my name to this list of illustrious writers. Indeed, the
whole experience, including my visit to the city, was
unforgettable.

The first thing I noticed on arrival in Limerick City, was
the fact that when the traffic lights go green there's more
than enough time to cross the road. I knew then this was a
place to be enjoyed at leisure, none of that frantic dash to
avoid being knocked down that I've encountered in lots of
places while trying to cross the road. A small thing you
might say, but for me it seemed to set the tone. The
readings are in the evening, so I took the time to explore
the many pleasures and treasures Limerick has to offer.

The Hunt Museum is a must see. Containing an
internationally important collection of approximately 2,000
works of art and antiquities, the museum is well worth

investing time in. Thanks to the generosity of John and Gertrude Hunt who collected the various works during their lifetime and donated them to the State, a visit begins in mounting enthusiasm and curiosity, ending in total appreciation and a sense of gratitude. What I really liked was the surprise element. As well as the many and varied works on show, there is the added bonus of opening drawers and finding paintings by artists such as Paul Gauguin or Renoir, an utter delight. Jack Butler Yeats and Roderic O'Connor are well represented, together with William Leach but indeed, every possible art form is catered to and every age, from medieval to modern.

I stayed at the Boutique Hotel on Denmark Street, a revelation in itself. The hotel has no foyer to speak of, but, like Alice's Adventures in Wonderland, it quirkily opens out and spreads itself for what seems like miles of red carpeted corridors.

The man behind the Wednesday evening reading, the chosen slot for writers to converge on the White House Bar on O'Connell Street, is Barney Sheehan, a legend in poetry circles for the encouragement and platform he has given to poets over the years. There's a touch of the theatrics about this gentle, courteous man, borne out by his smart suit and bowtie. Not to mention the red velvet curtained off stage set in a corner of the bar. I heard American voices and there was also a visitor from Malta, Robert Micallef, an academic who was on an Erasmus visit to Limerick. The world may seem large but you and I know it's very small indeed. I had great pleasure in telling Robert that my daughter was herself studying in Malta University on her Erasmus from Trinity College Dublin. We enjoyed a chuckle at the 'good of it!' I also met Gerard Siney who is spearheading a campaign, 'The Shannon Protection Alliance', in order to prevent the abstraction of 350 million litres of water from Lough Reagh on the River Shannon by

Dublin City Council. Gerard is currently* collecting poems about the Shannon and through the Alliance, is determined to do everything possible to prevent any action which might threaten the River Shannon. His passion for the river brought the poet Shelley to my mind when he said 'Poets are the Unacknowledged Legislators of the World'.

The format of the White House Poets is a successful one and one which will ensure it endures for a long time to come. As Clonmel poet Michael Coady once remarked at a poetry convention in Tallaght, 'Poetry is a feast and there is room for everybody at the table'. There is indeed space for everyone on the White House stage – the Open Mic at the beginning of the evening invites readings of new works in progress or recently published verse.

The White House Bar itself has a lovely retro quality to it, combining modern comforts with traditional furnishings. This lends an old fashioned feel to the place which isn't always a bad thing. I personally favour the sight of lots of warm wood instead of chrome and steel. En route to the rest rooms, down in the lower floors of the establishment, I saw a wonderful poster of one of Limerick's most famous sons, Richard Harris in his role as Gulliver in *Gulliver's Travels*. I was reminded that Limerick has produced many famous sons and daughters who went out into the world of art, literature and film and acquitted themselves with great credit.

I was fortunate enough to have met Frank McCourt twice in Dublin. The first was when he was signing *Angela's Ashes* and I said to him that I always wanted to write myself and my dream was to have my own book someday; 'Why aren't you doing it?' he barked back to me. He had a wicked gleam in his eye which quite threw me at the time. A few years later I saw him standing in Eason's on O'Connell Street, Dublin with his beautiful wife Ellen.

By then I had indeed published and wanted to tell him that he had spurred me on. Well, I did go and speak to him and he was genuinely delighted.

But to return to The White House Bar and the White House Poets' Platform. The night surely belongs to Barney Sheehan himself, Master of Ceremonies par excellence. He has a delightful delivery and manages to make everyone feel special. The fact that he writes poetry himself means he has total empathy with his invited guests and anyone who cares to come along and participate. Barney was born in Summerhill, Nenagh in 1934, moving to Limerick six months later. He claims to hold the record for selling the most tickets for any of Garryowen Rugby Club's fundraisers, no mean feat. As well as being a poet, he is also a craftsman using heraldic and medieval sculptured leather appliqué, a technique which he himself invented.

Before I left Limerick the next day, just when I thought it couldn't get any better, I wandered into Sean Kelly's bookshop on Little Catherine Street. Sean is also very connected to the White House Poets, being there right from the early days. But his passion for books and his determination to make his shop a place for the true lover of the written word is his main focus. It is a museum piece in itself. Old books, new books, in short, book heaven. As I sat on an old comfortable sofa, bathed in a ray of sunshine, I heard through an open window the magnificent sounds of violinist Luka busking his way through Vivaldi. I knew I would be going back and very soon.

*Since this piece was published, Gerard did indeed publish *Anthology for a River* (edited by Teri Murray) in association with Danu Press.

ONE FINE EVENING IN DALKEY
MEETING MAEVE BINCHY

We're nothing if we're not loved. When you meet somebody who is more important to you than yourself, that has to be the most important thing in life, really. And I think we are all striving for it in different ways. I also believe very, very strongly that everybody is the hero/heroine of his/her own life. I try to make my characters kind of ordinary, somebody that anybody could be. Because we've all had loves, perhaps love and loss, people can relate to my characters.

– Maeve Binchy

30 July as a calendar date is a significant one for lots of reasons; Baltimore, Maryland was founded (1729), Marseillaisian men sang the French national anthem for the first time (1792), Malden Island was discovered (1825), it concluded the Second Balkan War (1913) and the 10th modern Olympics opened in Los Angeles (1932). Alas, around the world the date will also resonate for another, sadder reason. It also marks the date of the demise of one of our most cherished writers, Maeve Binchy (1940–2012).

The extent of the outpouring of sincere grief and the amount of genuine tributes paid by such a large range of people from every walk of life is a fair indication of the esteem in which Maeve Binchy was held. She had superstar status right from the beginning, due mainly to her vivacity and captivating presence as a public speaker.

I remember going to hear her speak in Tullamore, County Offaly, way back in the early 1990s. I had taken the train with some friends and when we disembarked, there was Maeve on the platform, also having travelled down from Dublin by public transport. She seemed so ordinary, she had no airs or graces or anything like that. Later on that day, I remember her saying that writing a book was the easy part, speaking in public the hardest. No-one would ever guess she might suffer from nerves, such was her vibrant personality. She was just so entertaining, putting a smile on everyone's face.

Apart from the fact that she sold over forty million books worldwide (the best known of which are arguably *Circle of Friends*, *The Lilac Bus* and *Tara Road*), she was a charming, articulate, warm-hearted human being. Among the tributes that poured in after her death was a lovely affirmation by fellow writer Patricia Scanlan who said that Maeve was always very generous to her when she began developing her own career. Patricia is quoted in the *Evening Herald* as saying 'She was just so kind, normal and generous'.

When I read those words I cast my mind back to an evening in the mid 1990s. It was high summer and I was on my way to Dalkey with a group of new writers I was facilitating at the time in Ashfield College, Templeogue. We were on our way to Maeve's house and though we were in high spirits, deep down we were also very anxious. We wanted the evening to be a success and to acquit ourselves well. The jaunt to Dalkey came about because Maeve had been invited to come to Ashfield and talk to the writers as a special guest, for which she was also offered a fee. A letter came back politely declining the invitation on the grounds of ill health (her arthritis was bad at the time) but … and this was the miracle … if she couldn't come to us, she suggested that we could go to her house in Dalkey. There was no question of a fee either. And that's how we found ourselves in beautiful Dalkey, barely able to contain ourselves as we entered this gorgeous, picture postcard place. Every season provides its own feast. In winter, pale breasted brent geese can be seen making their passage from Dalkey to breeding grounds down the coast. Summertime brings glorious bursts of colour to gardens and of course, provides a haven for painted lady and red admiral butterflies.

When we arrived at Maeve's front door we rang the bell, expecting a servant to answer (after all, Maeve was rich and famous, adored by her public). Lo and behold, the great lady herself opened the door to us and the first thing we noticed was her smile. It seemed to beam on all of us equally; there was enough of its warmth to enfold everyone. We went inside and were shown through to her sitting room where wine and smoked salmon were set out on a table for us. Before we settled down for the evening however, she proved herself even more generous than we had hoped for. She brought us upstairs to a little roof garden full of flowers and also showed us the writing room specially built for herself and her husband Gordon Snell, also a writer. Side by side were the two desks over which each name was engraved on a plaque. Gordon is best known as a children's writer. All the while Maeve talked in such a witty, friendly way that we felt we had moved in and were now most definitely at home.

Not only had Maeve refreshments prepared for us but she had also prepared a tip-sheet, explaining first of all what kind of writer she was. She told us that there were writers who wrote stories and put them away in a drawer and came back months later and rewrote them. 'I wrote my stories in the morning and they were generally in the post in the afternoon', she said, with a lovely gleam in her eye.

Maeve Binchy may have made it all look so easy but it was because she had a natural affinity with human nature and understood what it was to experience the highs and lows of life. Three of the points she outlined that night still linger in my mind and I've often thought of them: Write about what you know, use your ear as a tape recorder, use your eyes as a camera. Great advice which stood her in great stead. When our evening came to an end, it was with regret we bade farewell but we had an enduring memory of a great night in a beautiful house and with a hostess much loved by so many. We were fortunate indeed. Years later I discovered that we both worked for the same college (Kilroy's College, Home Tuitions) as tutors, although at different times. May she rest in peace.

THE LEDWIDGE COTTAGE, SLANE

> When you come in, it seems a brighter fire crackles
> upon the hearth invitingly
> – 'To One Who Comes Now and Then', Francis Ledwidge

The Francis Ledwidge Cottage at Janeville, Slane is a fitting tribute to the memory of one of our most beloved national poets, a man of sensitivity, imaginative beauty, strength of mind and a powerful affinity with the natural world. These many and varied strands of a life cut short just before his thirtieth birthday are faithfully recreated within and beyond the walls of the cottage, thanks to the Ledwidge Cottage Committee.

The building itself is small as would be expected from a labourer's cottage where the poet's parents, Patrick and Ann (Lynch), first set up home in 1886. Just inside the front door stands a large shell, a chilling reminder of the price Ledwidge paid for joining the army in 1914. Having survived the horrors of Gallipoli and Serbia, Ledwidge lost his life during the third Battle of Yprés when a shell exploded beside where he stood drinking tea with the other men on road work. It was 31 July 1917.

I entered the cottage as a pilgrim in search of the many facets of the poet's life, which include son, brother, lover, soldier and poet. As I read the poems on display throughout the cottage written at various stages of the poet's life, the very walls themselves seemed to expand outwards from ordinary, domestic simplicity into the larger worlds of work, love and the devastating consequences of war.

It's a telling co-incidence in itself that the cottage contains four rooms, symbolising perhaps 'four green fields', for, although Ledwidge was a soldier in the British Army and fought in the First World War, he was a nationalist at heart. He gave as reason for enlisting:

> I joined the British Army because she stood between Ireland and an enemy common to our civilisation, and I would not have her say that she defended us while we did nothing at home but pass resolutions.

There were other reasons of course. A young man with a romantic sensibility, who had been rejected by the love of his life, Ellie Vaughey, was bound to feel a futility and a void which he quickly needed to fill. Ellie, who lived on a farm on the hill of Slane remained the love of Ledwidge's life right to the end. She was the inspiration for 'To One Dead', a particularly poignant poem and empathetic with the sadness that courses through his last works.

The objects and furnishings in the living areas are testimony to the simple life and pleasures that growing up in a large, impoverished family gave him. The table where meals were eaten, a dresser with its willow pattern delph and the settle bed to accommodate a large brood (Ledwidge was the second born of nine children) take up much of the small space. Arrayed on the shelf over the open fire are the items that bear witness to influences and simple pleasures he experienced as a child. An image of the Sacred Heart stands in pride of place beside an oil lamp, a well-worn shaving brush, a deck of playing cards which whiled away many a winter night and the fiddle that evokes the twilight playing of Matty McGoona. 'To One who Comes Now and Then' was written in honour of McGoona, Ledwidge's good friend.

On the window sill a bowl of flowers, although colourful and in season, seemed fragile, representing Ledwidge's unique relationship with nature, his understanding of the natural world and how this communion utterly informed his poetry. On the day I visited the wild selection included columbine (or Granny's bonnet) and sweet pea, both pixie-like in appearance. Ledwidge, as a young man, often found comfort in quiet places in a wood by the river Boyne, imagining the world of fairies and shape-shifting shadows.

Ledwidge is not a war poet recounting and retelling the horrific details of life on the battlefield and in the trenches. In that sense he is not in the tradition of Siegfried Sassoon or Rupert Brooke. In the bedroom of the cottage hangs a painting of a robin looking out across a vast, barren landscape. During the Third Battle of Ypres a lull in a bombardment allowed Ledwidge to hear the song of a robin. He wrote his loneliness into the lines:

> This is a song a robin sang
> This morning on a broken tree
> It was about the little fields
> That call across the world to me.
> – from 'Home'

The very same longing for home and hearth caused Ledwidge to pen 'Crocknaharna' en route to Gallipoli in the Dardanelles in 1915. The poem tells of the pangs of heartbreaking homesickness, associating the memory of his beloved mother, 'the pearl of Crocknaharna', with the place he loved so dearly. This attachment to the home place saw Ledwidge walking the thirty miles or so from Rathfarnham where he was apprenticed to a grocer when he was a young man of fifteen. This poem 'Behind the Closed Eye' speaks of walking 'the old frequented ways/That wind around the tangled braes'.

In the quarter acre garden at the back of the cottage a hazy carpet of bluebells fluttered in a gentle breeze. Overhead a blackbird's song rang out clearly over the landscape. Ledwidge is also known as 'Poet of the Blackbird', but here the song evokes a sense of melancholy in light of the trysting stone present in the garden, the stone which was taken from the Hill of Slane: it was where the poet used to meet his sweetheart Ellie Vaughey.

> A blackbird singing
> On a moss-upholstered stone,
> Bluebells swinging,
> Shadows wildly blown,
> A song in the wood,
> A Ship on the sea.
> The song was for you
> And the ship was for me.
> – from 'To One Dead'

Clearly, Francis Ledwidge was always thirsting for what was to elude him, contentment in the place of his birth and with the love of his life. Both were kept safe in his heart, right to the end.

A horse is the projection of peoples' dreams about themselves – strong, powerful, beautiful – and it has the capability of giving us escape from our mundane existence.

– Pam Brown

I was a yearling myself when Arkle was born in 1957 at Ballymacoll Stud in County Kildare. For the next thirteen years his heroic exploits on the racecourse seemed to enlarge the very proportions of our small two-up, two-down. My father, a quiet man at the best of times, waxed eloquent when talking about trainers, jockeys and the mysteries of the 'Dark Horse' that sometimes denied him the sure fire proceeds from a modest schilling investment. There were other great horses, of course, in this equine hall of fame, horses like Nijinsky for example, but it was Arkle's exploits on the racing field that first ignited my parents' shared passion for racing.

They grew animated when talking about his latest wins, and over the years his prowess as a champion provided them with plenty of winning betting slips. 'Arkle paid for those', mother said to me on my seventh birthday, handing me a much coveted pair of black patent shoes. My four-legged benefactor had won the Gold Cup, beating his arch rival Mill House into second place. Such munificence filled my parents with pride as if they, and not Anne Grosvenor,

Duchess of York, were the horse's owners. Arkle's trainer Tom Dreaper and jockey Pat Taaffe were also figures of legend and simply could do no wrong. Although my parents rarely left our midland town, in their imaginations they travelled every inch of those miles to the Curragh or further afield to Cheltenham when their hero was on the card.

At that time my father was the local postman, an early shift which saw him cycling all over the town on a big Rudge bicycle. He wore full uniform, navy gabardine with shiny buttons and a cap with a large glossy peak that resembled blinkers whenever he looked down. Returning from delivering the letters he always spoke of the weather in racing terms, the ground was either 'soft' or 'hard' and if ice covered the footpaths he'd say he nearly came a cropper at 'Breacher's Brook' on the slippery surface of a particular footpath.

Often on a Saturday, I accompanied my mother to the betting shop, or 'bookies' as she called it. While she poured over the racing pages tacked to the wall, I sat on the long wooden bench under thick frosted window glass, watching the bookmaker's assistant, a very glamorous lady with an Amy Winehouse upstyle, stamp down on the dockets with the full force of her elegant frame. As the floor grew more and more covered with balled-up dockets of defeat, my eyes fastened on this elegant creature, always dressed in twinsets and pearls. But it was her hands that fascinated me the most; her long fingernails varnished bright red were the same colour as her vibrant, lipsticked mouth. She gave out tiny pencils and yellow slips of paper with navy tracing paper between the layers, licking her index finger daintily before she took the top layer off the docket. My parents always held onto their dockets for a while after the races were over and the winners declared, just in case of a stewart's enquiry. Sometimes Ms O'Dwyer smiled at me benignly but other times she fastened me with a look of annoyance as if my staring fascination unnerved her.

Our radio had many humours also, its crackles and silences when results from Newmarket or Kempton were coming in saw my mother twiddling the knobs as if trying to unlock the combination of a safe. When all else failed I was despatched down the road to Jack the Cobbler whose kitchen smelt of leather and coal and whose radio was always crystal clear. We suspected that he listened to nothing else but racing results, never interfering with the tuning dial. Jack marked out the results with the stub of a pencil and then I'd speed home again, carrying the newspaper as if it were a sacred script. The markings could have been hieroglyphics for all I knew but made perfect sense to my parents.

Almost fifty years later I'm standing at the track in Keeneland, just outside Lexington. It's late January and the season will not begin until early April. Redwood trees are bare, the paddocks empty except for the brilliance of some cardinals, Kentucky's national bird, flitting around me. As a visitor to this state, I feel I owe it to my parents to at least come out and see some of the horse farms that bluegrass country is famous for. It's no accident that Lexington is twinned with County Kildare since 1985, a hands across the sea initiative began by President Dwight Eisenhower in 1956. Bluegrass country is beautiful whatever the season. Dry rock wall fences enhance the landscape and are poignant reminders of the many influences of the Irish immigrants that came here after frontier men like Daniel Boone in 1769 walked through the Cumberland Gap.

But here in Keeneland the scarlet of the cardinals remind me of crimson fingernails and as I gaze at the track I can imagine a capacity crowd hollering a favourite horse over the finishing line. Horses bred perhaps from

Kentucky's most famous equine, Man O'War, born in Fayette county and cast in bronze in monuments and plaques all over Lexington. Although this track is so far away from that midlands kitchen of long ago, I can well imagine my parents enjoying a fry up and debating what it is exactly that makes an enduring champion and which of these horses, Arkle or Man O'War, would nose ahead in their record books. The custom for burying a thoroughbred's heart, hooves and head is a well known one. Because of all the joy he gave to two people, who enjoyed simple pleasures, giving them a shared passion that lasted well into their later years, I've no doubt which of these horses I personally declare as having the most speed, intelligence and the biggest, most courageous heart.

THERE'S NO NEED TO FEAR THE WIND
IF YOUR HAYSTACKS ARE TIED DOWN
(old Irish proverb)

> Who is it that can tell me who I am?
> – William Shakespeare, *King Lear*

With a daughter in the house facing into the 2013 Leaving Certificate, it's not hard to remember my own experiences. With nearly four decades separating mother and daughter's Leaving Certificate odysseys, some things are bound to be different, while others remain the same.

William Shakespeare for one. *Macbeth* is the play for this year but the Bard of Avon also featured on the 1970s curriculum. How could I ever forget the effort it was to remember key passages from that epic work *King Lear*? Shakespeare set the hapless monarch the task of wanting to know which of his three daughters loved him the best. Luckily, I was living at home with my three sisters at the time. For the duration of the learning process, I imagined my siblings (named Philomena, Mary and Anne) as Lear's children, Goneril, Regan and Cordelia. I took them on board so much as royal personages that, long after the dreaded exam was over, it was months before I saw them as they truly were – young women with tie-died t-shirts, very wide flared trousers, large beehives and lots of hairspray. In fact, one of my sisters had a very noticeable kink in her fringe (a cow's lick) and spent a lot of time (and

Sellotape) trying to straighten it, a device that I'm sure William Shakespeare was not familiar with.

Often, when I should have been studying with all my might, my head was filled with music and wanting to go to dances with my siblings. While the midlands version of Goneril, Regan and Cordelia got ready for a night's jiving and quickstepping in the local hall, I was hunched over my books. I was a typical teenager for the times I suppose. On the one hand I wanted to do well and so I studied with great zeal. But on the other, my head was full of Horslips and Thin Lizzy. As a way of encouraging me to prepare, my mother would often cite the old Irish proverb, 'There's no need to fear the wind if your haystacks are tied down'.

As the day of the first exam in the Leaving Certificate drew near, the weather improved and the sun was literally splitting the stones; but I seemed to be forever stuck indoors. Back then, in the 1970s, the prize jobs were considered to be the bank or civil service. Mathematics was my weak subject and I knew I would have to try especially hard to even pass. Pythagoras and Euclid proved to be the twin pillars of my Leaving Certificate downfall. No matter how hard I tried, a positive outcome with regard to mathematics proved to be elusive. When I eventually sat the exam I was so nervous and had so many butterflies in my stomach that I wrote all the wrong answers. It was no surprise when the results came out and my worst fears were realised. I did well overall in most subjects but Pythagoras, the old rogue, had betrayed me.

As luck would have it, I decided to stay on at school for another year and complete a typing and shorthand course at the local technical college. I found that I actually enjoyed these subjects very much and they were the skills that eventually secured my first employment, in the typing pool at Heuston Station, Coras Iompair Éireann. I subsequently returned to education in 2000 opting for the long haul of a modular degree, the whole enterprise taking seven years to complete.

As a lifelong learner and part of a Grundtvig Adult Education Seminar initiative, I recently visited Odense, home of Hans Christian Andersen, one of the greatest writers of fairytales the world has ever known. Part of the trip included an excursion to a Folk High School at Ryslinge, situated on Fyn, only a short distance from the expressway between Odense and Svendborg. The ethos of the school reads like a fairytale in itself. Exams are prohibited. Creativity, innovation and early morning singing are the codes by which the Ryslinge Folk High School operates. The day of our visit was a particularly bright day and in response, finches, starlings and skylarks sang sweetly all over the grounds of this 150 year old establishment. It's a known fact that the increasing hours of daylight tempts the birds to sing, mirroring in a way what happens at the Folk High School. Here, students are allowed to brighten into their own voices in a nurturing atmosphere.

The Folk High School movement was founded in Denmark in 1830 by Nikolaj Frederick Severin Grundtvig who first and foremost recognised a need to provide a source of enlightenment for poor, uneducated peasants. The aim of enabling the passing on of knowledge and culture to Danish youth had as its primary goal the education of ambassadors who could return to their part of the country and create change. Grundtvig's philosophy is still practised today. In Folk High Schools this philosophy translates as a way of helping people become fully-rounded human beings as opposed to slavishly following conservative ideals of measuring ability solely through the exam system.

So whenever I see a really anxious frown on my daughter's face, I tell her to try her best, but not to make herself ill with worry either. I too cite the proverb my mother was so fond of, but when it comes to learning I now realise that tying down the haystacks of inner confidence and self worth are equally as important as anything found in books.

ALPINE MEMORY

It is better to go skiing and think of God, than go to
church and think of sport.

– Fridtjof Nansen

It's the month of July and I'm walking in the Penkens
overlooking Mayrhofen in the Zillertal Valley with my
husband of over thirty years. We breathe in the colours of
an august sky whose blueness seems to shimmer in
mountains rising up as far as the eye can see. By night
these baroque shapes are obliterated, inked out by
darkness, but we know they are there, we feel their
presence like a comforting shawl. By day they are veined
with narrow paths and tracks for walkers or more
adventurous climbers.

It's hard not to think of the genius of Mozart, born in the
city of Salzburg two hours away, or Julie Andrews singing
'The Hills are Alive', especially as we visited the birthplace
of the great composer the day before and enjoyed the
delights of the Mirabell Gardens. There Andrews do-ray
me-d her way around the red and yellow beauty of the
orderly flower beds. However, the strains we hear today
are the gentle swoon of sky-gliders overhead and bells
chiming the presence of brown cows with gentle faces.

Climbing for about forty minutes or so, we feel the ache
in our bones, especially the knee joints. It comes with the
territory of age. Walking in the Dublin Mountains, a
stone's throw from where we live, is not as challenging for

sure. Here the landscape glows with the white lustre of edelweiss and the ruby gems of alpinerosen, a scarlet rhododendron that reminds me of Killarney where my husband was born and reared. Yet this tranquil setting is also home to the Golden Eagle whose talons are lethal and who can spot his prey from one kilometre away. It's easy to forget that these mountains are stained with blood and have rung with the hunting cries of men like Emperor Maximilian, Ruler of the Holy Roman Empire.

It is said he always returned to the mountains and found comfort there and relief from the rigours of ruling the House of Hapsburg. Today however, with nothing sharper than the heels of our walking boots to threaten flora and fauna, we're heading for the restaurant up ahead, another ten minutes or so will take us there, our motivation, the stunning views and the coffee and apple strudel that awaits us.

Neither disappoint. We sit in the open air, cocooned in a silence where time itself stands still, opening its generous chasm, dropping a pearl from the past into the palm of an outstretched hand. I think back to only a week before when we boarded the bus at Innsbruck Airport that would take us to our holiday guesthouse in Mayrhofen, a jewel in the crown of the Zillertal Valley. Everything has gone to plan. In the distance I saw the outline of the Kitzbuhel mountains. They seemed to shield not only most of the sky but also provided a screen separating me, a middle-aged woman from the nineteen-year-old wisp of a girl I once was.

It's appropriate that the second time I come to Austria it is the end of summer and September beckons its season of mists and mellow fruitfulness. But in the spring of 1977, one year after the Winter Olympics were held in the Tyrolean capital, Innsbruck, I arrived with a group of young women, all of us working as shorthand typists with

Coras Iompair Éireann. Naturally, we wanted to avail of our free overland travel ... and gain an antidote to typing Van Hool McArdle type language all day, every day.

Back then the music in our heads came courtesy of Abba and The Bay City Rollers but we quickly adapted to the yodelling chorus in the après ski hours spent before a roaring log fire. It was indeed a long way from the typing pool in the offices above the train platforms at Heuston Station but, country girls all, we adapted very well. A long way too from the very basic bedsits we lived in around Rathmines and Clanbrassil Street. Rosy-cheeked from the fresh air, we learnt how to ski on the gentler slopes by day, our fitness levels severely tested and not found wanting. At night returning to our picture pretty wooden guesthouses, our exhausted but happy chatter barely concealed the crunch of snow underfoot. The moon beamed down on the snow-glazed paths, shiny with crystals.

On the Penken Mountains, while my husband closes his eyes to catch a sly forty winks, that girl flashes before me in her yellow cardigan and maroon bellbottoms, her eyes bright and laughter bubbling up within her. I wonder how much of her is still within me? Would she have marvelled at the splendour of Maximilian's Golden Roof, an architectural highlight in Innsbrook, or spent an entire afternoon pondering on Archduchess Maria Theresa's grief when her husband Francis Stephen dies suddenly at his son's Leopold's wedding? I close my eyes and imagine myself at nineteen on the ski slopes. My cheeks are pink with exhilaration and the prospect of a cosy evening by a log fire in good company. That girl, back then, certainly didn't know that some day she would have her own dynasty, two sons and two daughters.

One thing for sure, I'm eternally grateful that the opportunity for such an unforgettable experience came my way when it did because it fills me with joy each time I relive it.

When my husband nudges my elbow, telling me we better start making our way back to the bright yellow ski-lift that will take us down again to the valley, I can't help but smile. The words of Ralph Waldo Emerson come to me: 'The years teach much which the day never knew'.

DRIVING DE VALERA'S CAR

We cannot afford idleness, waste or inefficiency.
— Éamon de Valera

There's something about a vintage vehicle that ignites the glamour engine. Think David Hasselhoff's plush Pontiac in *Knight Rider* or the sleek mobile of the stars, favoured by legends such as Elvis and sung into rockabilly history by Sammy Masters in his 1950s classic 'Pink Cadillac'.

My family didn't own a car when I was growing up in the 1960s. Vintage or otherwise. A fun car like the Volkswagen Beetle of *Herbie* fame or a tasty Mustang were as far removed from us as the Great Wall of China. As was the possibility of owning a revved-up Chevrolet like the one Dr Emmett Brown converted into a time machine in the film *Back to the Future*. Like most other families in the street we relied on our two pins or 'shank's mare'. Outings to places outside of town boundaries were usually confined to sites of pilgrimage like Knock Shrine. We then boarded Dolan's red and white tour bus, air-conditioning provided by every window being left wide open; ensuring we arrived with our hair wired to our skulls. Those excursions usually involved lots of lukewarm lemonade and plenty of ham sandwiches.

I recently read that de Valera's Dodge Plymouth has undergone a restoration project having suffered in 2009 the effects of heavy flood damage to the display room at Ennis

Museum where the car is usually on show. The news of the restoration brought me back a few years to when I first visited the museum and made my debut behind the wheel of a celebrity vintage vehicle. Although high summer and swallows were seriously thinking of heading south, there was still glorious colour about, thanks to bursts of wild poppies and tall gladioli. A friendly, holiday atmosphere in Ennis town ensured there was firm suspension under the bounce in my step as I made my way to Ennis Library.

Before long, I'm admiring de Valera's 1947 Dodge Plymouth, purchased by him from Sean T. Ó Ceallaigh in 1959 for an undisclosed sum when Ó Ceallaigh stepped down as President of Ireland. The car has been housed at the de Valera Library museum in Ennis since 1988 after being passed onto the local council by his descendents. Black and sleek-skinned as the cheeky otter who peered up at me an hour or so earlier from the river Fergus, I could almost see my face reflected in the paintwork. Solid, dependable and very masculine looking, the car was built in Detroit by Chrysler. The engine is capable of almost 62 miles per hour. I sought permission to sit inside the classic vehicle and was soon savouring the spaciousness of a car that is 75 inches wide, 66 inches in height and 226 inches long. These generous dimensions reminded me that de Valera himself was nicknamed 'The Long Fellow', because of his great height. There was certainly plenty of room for him to fold those stilt-like legs in a car that has the capacity to carry a driver and eight passengers. My hands grip a smooth steering wheel devoid of any identifying marks, unlike the Skylark, an anniversary model Buick bought by Bob Hope in the fifties. Hope had his name inscribed in the steering wheel as a status symbol.

What would de Valera think of me enjoying this cool interior with nothing remotely resembling politics on my mind? And in the driving seat no less of a car that had transported him the length and breadth of Ireland during his presidency? Cream-coloured leather upholstery and the wooden casing around the dash, radiated Hollywood grandeur. It's no surprise de Valera purchased it, being of American stock himself.

Driving de Valera's car, I close my eyes, morphing into Marilyn Monroe, oozing sequins and feather boa. I'm out on the main road, the window open, wind ruffling luxurious curls through my hair, singing 'I want to be loved by you'; the car's registration ZH 1333 being memorised by envious onlookers as I cruise through towns and villages where comely maidens once danced. Everyone pauses in whatever they are doing to guess what VIP is passing through. I'm not exactly certain where I'm headed but I imagine somewhere swanky, Ennis's answer to the Algonquin in Manhattan perhaps or some other venue worthy of such a vehicle. For those magical moments, it never even enters my head that the car is stationary, the engine cold.

Even day-dreams run out of steam. Before I vacate the car, I have a photograph taken by the kind-hearted museum attendant using my 'vintage', non-digital camera. Days later, when I see the print, the movie star expression on my face says it all. Included in the photograph are the highly-polished shoes of Éamon de Valera, all that could be seen of his poster image on the wall behind the car captured in the rear view mirror. I'm glad that de Valera's face doesn't feature. I'm not completely certain his eyes would register approval at the journey I brought his faithful Dodge Plymouth on, that high summer day in Ennis.

A Scarlett Moment

No, I don't think I will kiss you, although you need
kissing, badly. That's what's wrong with you. You
should be kissed and often, and by someone who
knows how.

– Rhett Butler

Virginia born Lady Astor, a former member of the British
Parliament, once described Savannah as 'a beautiful lady
with a dirty face'. However, when I visited the city that
General Sharman captured on his march to the sea, this old
bastion of the south never looked lovelier. It's many years
ago since I walked those gorgeous magnolia-lined
pathways, but I can still see the gentle sway of
extravagantly-festooned ballgowns and crinolines, shaped
in the sweep of Live Oaks trimmed with the feathers of
Spanish moss. Azealeas and camellias gleamed their
brilliance in shady nooks and, although a respectably-
married woman, the dormant coquette in me soon sprang
to life.

One such opportunity presented in a photographer's
window display on River Street. For a few dollars and a
little confidence, I could be captured for all time as an
authentic southern belle, resplendent in rustles of taffeta –
with ruffles of lace at wrist and hem. Pantaloons and
parasol were also on show and on a nearby table, the
spread fan that is the stock in trade of every flirt worth her
salt. A portrait of Vivienne Leigh in her role as Scarlett

O'Hara drew my lingering gaze. Although Scarlett chose Atlanta instead of Savannah in order to escape the boredom of Tara, the lush, intoxicating perfume drifting from the many magnolia blossoms throughout the city brought her presence keenly.

Gazing at the southern belle ensemble, I wrestled with temptation. The plunging neckline reminded me how Scarlett's faithful old Mammy advised her wilful charge that it just wasn't seemly for a lady to reveal her bosom before three o'clock in the afternoon. Despite this prescription on how to be a lady, part of me wanted to shed my boring summer cottons and transform myself into a minx with nothing in her head but the riddle of an unresolved love affair.

However, I soon realised that having 'A Scarlett moment' ran a little deeper than a sly smile and a haughty tilt of a dimpled chin. Was I really up to the O'Hara challenge? As a woman of mature years, did I truly possess enough insight into her feisty, devious nature? Not to mention her mental agility when scheming to steal the object of her affections, Ashley Wilkes, from his sweetheart Melanie. Could I, for instance, have ever stooped so low?

But of course, the truth of the matter was that the young girls I palled around with as a teenager were much more robust than poor Melanie Wilkes who wouldn't say boo to a goose! Heaven help me if I'd tried to muscle in on any of those lassies' beaux at the local dances. In fairness, however and although there weren't any swashbuckler types insisting that I needed to be kissed, and often, and by someone who knew how; I did indeed manage, on occasion, to arrive home with delicious after shocks of kissing on my lips. But was that enough?

For one thing, I'd never worn a dress that first saw life rolled on a large bolt and displayed in a fabric shop. A dress that was subsequently fashioned with the expertise of a Coco Chanel, having been ripped from a curtain pole. Transforming material from such humble beginnings into every best dressed gal's 'must have' for the current season surely could only happen in the world of celluloid? In the movie, Scarlett's famous green velvet number, especially designed by Walter Plunkett for the film version of the book, was put together with not an inch of Velcro in sight. And I've never had a nineteen inch waist, even with the aid of the most cunning engineering corsetry has to offer. Whereas it was considered good breeding in southern belle etiquette to eat like a bird, I've always had the appetite of a plough horse, especially when it comes to dumplings or apple pie. Languishing on a gingham picnic cloth with a rumbling belly while feigning a full stomach was simply never an option.

The fact that I was born and bred in the same Irish Georgian town in the midlands of Ireland that John Stephens left in 1833 to join an older brother in the United States didn't cut me any mustard either. In 1863, Stephens, of a good Catholic gentry family married Annie Fitzgerald, the daughter of Philip Fitzgerald and his wife Eleanora McGhan of Rural Home, Clayton County, Georgia. Annie Fitzgerald, Margaret Mitchell's paternal grandmother, is thought to have provided the inspiration for *Gone with the Wind*'s passionate heroine. But the midlands thread is a very tenuous one and easily unravelled.

Just as I was beginning to despair of getting under the skin of the true Scarlett experience, I heard the shrill sound of a steamboat's calliope as it made its way upriver. It was then I remembered Knock in County Mayo, where, at the age of sixteen, I was the beneficiary of male interest in the form of a piercing wolf whistle.

I had just alighted from Dolan's tour bus, having spent the journey listening to sporadic recitations of the rosary, eating ham sandwiches and drinking lukewarm lemonade.

I remember the day of the excursion as being very hot. Golden sunshine bounced off the tour bus windows and all the ladies' perms drooped limp against damp foreheads. Coats were quickly discarded but in deference to our 'Irish summer' we still had plenty of 'casing' with heavy cardigans and jumpers. However, with a yellow rim of lemonade around my mouth and a fair sprinkling of crumbs on my jersey, appreciation from a virile young male, at such a high pitch, hadn't featured on my list of expectations. The youth in question was sitting on bags of spuds on the back of a truck. 'A bould pup' my mother described him to her cronies while my cheeks burned with a colour deeper even than the red petticoat bought by Rhett Butler for Scarlett's Mammy.

Despite my initial embarrassment at the 'bould pup's' appreciation, I soon formulated the plan that provided the means of escaping to the town. Not long after the parked bus relaxed down on its fat wheels, I pretended a queasiness from the journey which belied my ox-like constitution and I gave a swooning Oscar standard performance that Vivienne Leigh would have been proud to own. After pleading a need for fresh air, I was allowed to remain outside the Basilica and as soon as the last of our group disappeared inside, I was off down the town in search of my hero. There I strolled nonchalant yet eager to give that young buck the glad eye should we meet on terra firma. Unfortunately, that's where the plan fell foul. When I did see the young man lounging against the tailboard of the spud truck, he was already engaged in animated discussion with another belle who wore seamed stockings and a much shorter skirt than my own. I realised that, although tomorrow may well have been another day, it wasn't likely to make much difference as far as I was concerned.

In the end, on that day in Savannah, after much wrestling with my 'inner Scarlett', I chose not to enter the photographer's studio on River Street, even though I was completely satisfied that I had indeed passed the Scarlett test.

FOREST BATHING ON LA GOMERA

I like living. I have sometimes been wildly, despairingly, acutely miserable, racked with sorrow, but through it all I still know quite certainly that just to be alive is a grand thing.

– Agatha Christie

In February 1927, Agatha Christie went to the Canaries to recover from psychological strain. Her mother, Clarissa Miller had died after a severe illness, her husband was in love with another woman and she was going through a period of financial difficulties. She stayed at the Gran Hotel Taoro in Puerto de la Cruz, the best hotel in Tenerife at that particular time. It is said that while there, Agatha Christie completed *The Mystery of the Blue Train*, a book which sold so well it ended her money worries. She then relocated to Las Palmas de Gran Canaria where she stayed at the Metropole Hotel where she wrote 'The Companion', one of the mysteries included in her collection of short stories, *The Thirteen Problems*. In 'The Companion', one of the characters says of the Canary Islands: 'They must be wonderful', while another makes the remark 'The Peak of Tenerife is a fine sight with the setting sun on it'.

It's easy to imagine a writer like Christie being so inspired by what she experienced, being inspired enough to begin writing again. The light is so very different, almost golden in its brightness, one can't but feel well. No wonder films such as *Wonderful Life* (a 1964 film starring Cliff Richard) was filmed on the famous sand dunes at Maspalomas. Painters too adore the quality of such glorious illumination.

La Gomera is my own personal favourite. My principal reason for visiting there was to admire the natural terrain but also to walk in Garajonay National Park, the home of the lauisilva or laurel forest, formed by a multitude of different plant species. The park is made up of a wide variety of evergreen trees all thriving in an atmosphere of high humidity with a fairly constant year round temperature. On the southern slope the forest is dominated mainly by heather and fayatrees, two species which are better able to cope with the dryer atmosphere. In places where mist tends to form you will often find tiny plants with twisted trunks that are completely covered in moss and lichen. The park is extremely accessible since it is crossed by numerous tracks and footpaths linking the various villages and hamlets scattered around the island.

I had heard of the health benefits of 'Forest Bathing', a concept which originated in Japan (where it's called shinrin-yoku). Dr Qing Li, one of the main researchers in this field, identified the healing ambience of walking in a forest as a huge boost for the immune system and a great way of lowering blood pressure. Inhaling the forest's essential oils from wood and enjoying a range of sensory perceptions overall leaves the forest 'bather' with renewed health benefits.

I've walked in forests in Ireland – Avondale Forest Park at Rathdrum, County Wicklow is exquisite. Birr Castle Demesne is one of my favourite places on the planet. It boasts Ireland's oldest tree, 200 years old, alas felled by storms in early 2014. Avondale is noted for its exotic trees, including Hornbeam, Norway Sitka Spruce, European Oak and West Red Cider. Thanks to Augustine Henry (1851–

1930), there is such a wide variety on offer. Henry was a pioneer when it came to realising the potential of scientifically-managed forests. Yet, there's something close to mystical about the experience of walking in Garajonay National Park. The plateau that occupies the central highland area of La Gomera is, for most of the year, covered with a blanket of mist that is blown by the wind into different directions and often spills down into the southern region of the island. Shrouded and protected by this magical sea of clouds is the dense evergreen forest that is Garajonay.

The wide variety of trees thriving here exist in an atmosphere of high humidity with a fairly constant year round temperature. The more humid and sheltered valleys to the north contain the lushest part of the forest, a true subtropical jungle. In the higher altitudes the forest loses some of its more delicate species. Queen of the Mountain (Ixanthus Viscosus), a woody bush with yellow flowers, grow in the shadier parts of the laurel forest. The flora in this region is perfect for 'Forest Bathing' as it encompasses around twenty species of woodland plants and 47 endemic varieties. Indeed, the area's original settlers were more forest people than village dwellers and survived by raising livestock, collecting wood to make charcoal and using the natural properties of local plants to make healing infusions and hand-carving wooden utensils. Wildlife, despite being a little more difficult to see in the dense forest areas is nevertheless equally interesting.

All of the trails in Garajonay National Park are well mapped out, to include estimated time taken for the walk, its degree of climbing/descent and what natural delights are on offer for savouring. On the trail from Agando Rock to Santiago Beach by way of Benchijigua, for example, the geography of the walk is mapped out through visual clues in the landscape; large pine trees, groves of eucalyptus.

The most well-trodden route, however, is to be found on the northern side of the park. One of the trails, from Cruz de Tierno to Vallehermoso by way of Cano rock, measures just over four and a half kilometres and makes for a very pleasant downhill stroll which takes around one and three-quarter hours. Cano rock is visible through most of the walk as it rises majestically into the sky. The park has four recreational areas and there is also a special area for campers. How did I feel after my walk in such lush surroundings? Wonderful. I felt I had indeed 'bathed' in beauty, totally restored in mind and body.

A FASCINATION WITH FABRIC

> I caught a startled glimpse of the woman then, her
> own dreams stitched in the red silk.
> > – Eileen Casey, 'My Mother's Hands'

I've always been drawn to the painting 'Woman in a
Striped Dress', by Édouard Vuillard (1868–1940). Apart
from its obvious visual vivacity, layers of meaning nestle
in this soft, almost buttery post-Impressionistic work.
Vuillard lived with his widowed mother in Paris until she
died when he was aged sixty. She was a dressmaker and a
self-proclaimed muse for the French artist. So many
elements in this painting remind me of my 1960s
childhood, growing up in a house where my mother too
was a dressmaker and a lasting influence on my creative
life. The fusion of two women in the foreground of the
painting, while a young girl emerges in the background,
reveal the various stages of the female form in physical
and psychological terms. While there's a great sense of
unity, the women appearing to 'bloom' together, there's
also the very real feeling of being worlds apart.

In 1952, hoping to supplement the family income, my
mother bought a Singer sewing machine. The purchase
immediately established her as a seamstress in our street.
All these years later, although the machine is long gone,
we still have the receipt. It cost twenty six pounds, three
schillings and three pence, but because it was bought on an

instalment plan, the actual cost was thirty pounds, seven schillings and sixpence. The receipt bears the stamp of the Singer Sewing Machine Company and was purchased from Fayle's Hardware Shop in Birr town. Back then it was an awkward looking contraption unlike its more streamlined sisters of today. All steel and delicate rosewood, it was placed in the parlour and permanently occupied the space beneath the net curtains of our small window.

Mother's skills in the beginning were of a more practical nature; she soon became adept at prolonging the wear in a garment. She could turn the jaded collar of a shirt or, through the refinement of a false hem, add another year to an almost outgrown school uniform. The type of work she did appeared to mirror the financial circumstances of the street. Men who hadn't emigrated to England were largely out of work, women were expert at making money stretch. Most young people left school at the age of fourteen, but mother was adamant that would not be the fate of her brood, six of us in total. It meant that while on the one hand I could stay in school and keep pursuing the subjects I loved (English and History), I was immediately separated from the pals I grew up with. While they headed towards the factories (Dubarry Shoes or Moquette Fabrics), in high heels and wearing lipstick, I trailed after them, shapeless in my navy serge uniform and light blue blouse. At the time, it felt strange and more than a little unsettling. Like the young girl in Vuillard's painting, I was very much an outsider.

The last sound I'd hear before falling asleep was the steady treadle of the wheels as the sewing machine earned its keep. Muffled behind the closed door of our parlour, it was a comforting rhythm which seemed to come from a million miles down the hallway in our two-up, two-down council house. I'd fall asleep imagining a blur of cloth and hands as the fabric inched through my mother's fingers. Whatever the enterprise, it was pleasing to know that shapeless bundles of cloth were slowly gaining a new lease of life. Because of the paraphernalia of the sewing, the house often appeared very disorganised, with a medley of materials jostling for space with old newspapers and the general rough and tumble of a growing family living in a confined space. Again, a reminder of Vuillard's painting which drew inspiration from the claustrophobic nature of family life, the cluttered settings which suggest the conflict of interior worlds and the burden of words left unsaid.

Fabrics, in various stages of evolution, were draped over chairs or flowed like a river from the machine, transformations sometimes interrupted by my mother's other domestic duties. She was also constrained by having to sew in the evening. My father worked as a night telephonist and then delivered the first morning post. Anything remotely connected with noise was undertaken when he was out of the house. He spent most of the afternoon into evening sleeping, in preparation for his own world of work. We crept around the house or played outdoors but come nightfall, the house became amplified.

It fell to me to deliver the finished articles to mother's clients. Those long hours she spent at the machine were represented by anonymous brown parcels I distributed after school. I don't know how she could have made a profit out of this enterprise but our popularity with the neighbours was assured. Also, she'd give me strips of gabardine, or serviceable serge, to crudely shape into dolls clothes. Through these fragments, I was entering the transcendent world of imagination.

However, I secretly longed for the glamour of softer, shinier material. This did not happen until mother finally came into her own, when she began to receive commissions for dance frocks. There was an upturn in the economics of the street, older girls in the neighbourhood were working on 'piece rate' and could afford the luxury of dances and showbands. They purchased remnants in local drapery shops, asking her to convert them into coveted designs seen in magazines. She seldom let them down, using old newspapers to make individual patterns. That itself was a feat of engineering, but she had a keen sense of proportion and where the various points of adjustment should be. Her patterns catered for the larger as well as the smaller ladies. Then, on our kitchen table she'd make the first incisions, shearing neat waistlines or cursing the glare of polka dot or stripe, both of which were hard on her vision and sometimes caused spots to swim before her eyes. Although she might complain about the flimsiness of fabric, its unsuitability for one reason or another, she did her very best to produce the dream creation.

When the time for fittings came, the young women shucked off drab, colourless factory smocks as if they were shedding old skin. The scent of their perfume, the glitter of sequences or flamboyant trims, was indeed a heady mixture. All the latest hits poured from our radio: Joe Dolan or the Clipper Carlton were among the background music selection, while talk focused on the rustle of taffeta or the wide flare of a dirndl skirt, how it might swing for the quickstep. If the interior lives in Vuillard's painting were repressed, that wasn't the case as mother pinned and tucked the fabric around flesh and blood mannequins. There was something about the process that brought forth secrets and confidences. Street gossip was large on the agenda and at an early age I discovered the shorthand for betrayals, unexpected pregnancies and worst of all, miscarriages. Sometimes, on a spontaneous burst of excitement I'd be swung up out of my chair by girls I'd played 'chainies' with (a game of shop with broken china) in the laneways behind our houses. A temporary jiving partner, I was re-united with them once more while the soar of a saxophone quickened through our pulses.

Also, an added bonus was that I now had the leftover scraps from these dresses, scraps that I still collected, which glowed like jewels in the box I kept them in. Mother would smile, forging a conspiratorial bond between us, as she handed me the salvage. Although my mother tried to teach me, I never did learn to sew, being much too clumsy with a needle to ever master the art. As a consequence of that time in my life, in the 1960s, I can never resist the lure of fabric; its power to bring the exotic into the most ordinary of places. Mother loved her garden also, a very congested area, filled with geraniums, begonias and fuchsia bells. It became her principality when she was outdoors. This earthiness too is reflected in Vuillard's painting, the vibrant russet and white stripes on the woman's dress evocative of furrows in a field. But most of all, it's the hands depicted in the painting that speak to me the most, bringing my mother's labours to the fore and how they shaped the light and shade of my life.

She had the hands of a countrywoman
hands that reached deep into the earth,
had known the ache of bloated cows at milking,
were gentle with the new-born chicks of spring
long before a wedding ring embedded in her flesh
taking her to where houses grew in place of corn.
She did not mourn the past, brought it with her;
her hands found roots in the new soil.

She never hid her hands, never wore gloves
to mass on Sundays.
In child dreams I dressed them in satin,
smoothed the knotted knuckles into slender stems,
made them fragile as a flower

not seeing then the beauty they possessed
how they fashioned the living truth of what she was.

On my sixteenth birthday she surprised me with a dance frock.
I watched as cloth and hands made perfect partners
saw it dip through her fingers before spinning
to a coloured pool at her feet.
I caught a startled glimpse of the woman then,
her own dreams stitched in the red silk.

– from 'My Mother's Hands'

Soot

If a lump of soot falls into the soup and you cannot conveniently get it out, stir it well in and it will give the soup a French taste.

— Jonathan Swift

In the house where I was born the only form of heating was the open fire which was always in use during long winter months – usually from the end of October right through until the following spring. Bales of briquettes and bags of turf were purchased from huge trucks that came into the street on a monthly basis.

At the time of my growing up, there was a saw mill in the town. Our fathers bought 'bogey' loads of timber in the summer and hauled them home by hand, with more than a little help from neighbours. As a result, our back garden often resembled a fuel merchant's depot. Such was the fear of cold winters that every spare penny went on fuel and food. Pots of stew and warm grates were the order of the day. There's a famous quote from Hubert H. Humphrey the American Vice President under Lyndon B. Johnson that often comes to my mind when thinking about the 'smoking' chimneys of that midland street. Humphrey said:

There is in every American something of the old Daniel Boone who, when he could see smoke from another chimney, felt himself too crowded and moved further out into the wilderness.

It was the exact opposite in that street of terraced houses. Once the first wispy trail of black rose from one chimney, the rest followed until it looked as if a tribe of American Indians had moved in and were sending frantic smoke signals to each other at every hour of the day or night.

About every two years, when the smoke began to billow out into the parlour, floating little black balloons on the armchairs and picture rail, father would announce his intention to clean the chimney. I say announce because as he'd so often declare: 'Rome wasn't built in a day'. He certainly had nothing in common with Dick Van Dyke's character Bert in *Mary Poppins*, breaking into 'Chim Chim Cher-ee' at the drop of a broom and dancing over the rooftops with alacrity. I suppose it's easy to understand why. The houses were tiny, families were large and anything at all that disrupted the day to day had to be planned out. For one thing, the fire would be out of commission and for another, all the furniture and curtains would have to be covered in old sheets and plastic. Because the houses were in a terraced row, the chimney system seemed to be interconnected like the wires in the telephone exchange my father worked in. If one chimney needed unblocking, then the inhabitants of the adjoining two-up, two-down, felt the effects also. Therefore, it was usually on the insistence of next door that the cleaning would eventually be carried out.

Mother always kept a supply of old flour bags. They were very serviceable and came in handy for lots of cleaning jobs. We owned our own set of brushes but more often than not they were on loan to a neighbour. Ownership sometimes had to be vigorously re-established before they were returned. The smell of smoke perpetually clung to those brushes and father always shook them out at the back of the garden before bringing them indoors. He'd joke that we should brush our teeth with the black powder, that it would save him a fortune in toothpaste, and we'd scream out in horror, imagining ourselves with black teeth and foul breath. We also knew about the neighbour a few streets away who'd had the bright idea of tackling a blocked chimney from the top down as it were instead of the bottom up. He'd left a large sack taped around his grate and his masterplan was that the soot would shoot downwards and fall into the sack which would then be neatly tied up and disposed of. Easy peasy! Not so. The poor man shoved the chimney brushes down the wrong chimney pot and flooded his neighbour's parlour with an unexpected blizzard! This 'chimney' story had gone into our family lore and was dusted off each time our own chimney was cleaned. But we'd scarcely have time to enjoy it such was the work in hand.

We taped an old board with a hole in it over the fireplace and spread our flour bags all over the floor and furniture. Mother stood staunchly by father's side, handing him each rod to be screwed onto the next and helping him give a great whoosh upward. Both of them would have tied old scarves around their noses and mouth to avoid breathing in too much smoke. We'd be posted outside and instructed to tap on the window when the bristle, shaped like a horned beam crown appeared out of the chimney pot. That was the eureka moment. All that had to be done then was to pull back on the rods and try to contain the black downpour.

It was always a surprise to see the powdery mountain which was shovelled up (again into flour sacks) and taken outside to be spread over the back garden as a sort of compost – very good for onions father often said, even though we had no onions!

Nowadays, chimney cleaning is so much more efficient. The modern sweep dressed in sturdy overalls has the room prepared and the soot vacuumed up in jig time. I'm glad however that I held onto those chimney brushes, now stored in a shed in a housing estate in Tallaght. They bring to mind two beloved faces. Despite my parents' best attempts at staving off the particles that lodged around their eyes and mouth, each powdery crevice is captured in memory like a charcoal drawing. The brushes also bear the earthy, distinctive smell of soot, reminding me of fires that burned through winter evenings long ago.

LETTER TO MY DAUGHTER

> And so our mothers and grandmothers have, more
> often than not anonymously, handed on the creative
> spark, the seed of the flower they themselves never
> hoped to see – or like a sealed letter they could not
> plainly read.
>
> – Alice Walker

There, it's gone off again, making a buzzing sound like an alarm clock. I know by the brightness flashing from your eyes, the pink glow on your cheeks, that there is a message on your mobile from that 'special' someone. A message that makes you oblivious to my presence here at the kitchen table writing what you probably imagine is a dull shopping list.

No doubt you are thinking that such a middle-aged matron as I am would not appreciate the urgency of these text messages or the need to reply so immediately. Or the speed of technology. I can't blame you on that score; it took me ages to resist using the mobile. I'm so glad that you insisted I learn, it was a piece of cake once I picked up on it. And to be able to text you when you're out eases a lot of the worry of these teenage years.

Your fingers fly along, deft as the finest concert pianist, making your own peculiar notes, abbreviations no doubt for the language of love. I know. And you have told me so often I mustn't be so old fashioned. L.v., though a consonant and a vowel short, still stands for the word 'love'. And I am so much older than you, my darling, my first-born daughter coming to me after such a long gap after the birth of your two brothers who are now full-grown men and married themselves.

Yet I was sixteen once upon a time and beautiful too, as you are now. My hair was long and glossy and I was always listening to music on the radio. We didn't have iPods or earphones or anything like that. Instead my fingers flew across pages and pages like winged messengers trying to keep up with my thoughts. My thoughts were speedy and I was lifted airborne by the magical world of love. How could I ever forget that heady time?

You see I too had my first real boyfriend at age sixteen. We had no telephones or texting machines then. Our thoughts were hourly filled with each other but there was no quick way of communicating those thoughts. No abbreviations, no shorthand. And just as well because the memories of getting those letters are still very vivid. You see he lived on a farm outside the town. As a result he was very close to nature and was very appreciative of the seasons and their meanings. From him I too learnt to savour the changing colours of the year and I looked for the coming and the going of the swallow, that tiny little bird that so bravely makes such a long and hard journey every year to our shores.

Although the object of my heart's desire travelled in from outside the town and I saw him at lunch times and briefly after school, most weekends were endless without sight of him. Yet love finds a way. His cousin worked in one of the larger bakery shops in the town and most Saturdays this cousin would bring in a package for me from my sweetheart which I, or your grandmother, would collect. Mostly your grandmother did because she was up so early and out getting the shopping in while I was still dreaming sweet dreams. Like you, dear daughter, I always needed that extra hour.

But just imagine! There, under a counter bursting with fresh-made bread and delicious cakes, that parcel waited to be collected. When she'd return from the town, your grandmother would wake me up and my first sight of the day was that brown paper parcel secured with string or strong Sellotape. Barely awake I'd tear open the prize to find a book recently finished and much enjoyed and passed on for me to share. There was an indefinable sense of that package being wrapped at a table late at night, sprinkled with moon dust or folded together in the early morning when the day was only beginning.

But the biggest prize of all would be the letter that tumbled out of the centre of the book. That letter would be read and reread and the whole world was made fresh again as I savoured each line, each word, going over it and over it. Those words wound around my heart like a soft, silky breeze. All those envelopes, full of letters written in quiet moments at windows filled with canopies of sky or leaf and birdsong. All those pages covered with such strong handwriting were kept in a drawer beside my bed. What other treasures need I have wished for?

First love is so special. But first love isn't always the one that lasts. I still think of that kind, gentle boy with much fondness but as the months passed, like the seasons, our romance changed. One day I opened your grandmother's range and burnt those letters and I knew that it was right that ashes were all that remained of a romance grown cold. I still had a good friend at the end of it all, however, and fine preparations for when I eventually met your father some years later.

I had come to Dublin to work in Heuston Station as a typist. Your father was very young also but our homesickness and loneliness was less sharp when we caught sight of each other one evening, both of us walking home to our bedsits along the canal that, as luck would have it, were literally around the corner from each other. The hours didn't seem quite so long in the typing pool after those glimpses, though it was quite a while before I plucked up the courage to say hello one summer evening.

Your father had the most beautiful raven black hair, black as black could be. He was born and reared under the nestling presence of Torc Mountain in Muckross, Killarney, a place full of the passion and wildness of nature. That evening when I said hello, I was rewarded by a wonderful smile that swept away all thoughts of loneliness for my own home, a small town in the midlands. We were drawn to each other, two lonely young people not long left home, a loneliness that we eventually put down into words when the letters between us began to be written on various occasions over the years. Letters that often returned to those times when we first met. How else could we have expressed those early days of love and longing? Of trying to find ourselves in the strangeness of a city landscape?

Sometimes there is only the white space on a page that is like a silence which, when broken, can only say exactly what you want to say. A line of words rippling into another as the fishing line is reeled out onto the water, finding the deepest part of the lake, bringing the 'catch' to shore, glinting in the light. On those pages I still can see the sheen of your father's dark hair, as it was then, and the blueness of his eyes, as they still are. And the stretch upwards of his tall, lean frame.

On those pages, your father's Kerry lilt perfectly compliments your mother's midlands brogue, in the same way as mountains compliment flat landscape. Your father, coming from a place abundant with mountains and lakes, was the perfect companion for a young woman reared so near the bog. He used to joke that my brown eyes had shades of turf in them! On those white pages, between those lines laid like a track, were journeys I never dreamed of, journeys I savour each time they are read and re-read. I learn again of your father's big, wide generous heart, of his own loneliness, fading like the night sky once we became sweethearts, a love that has lasted over thirty years. I still hear the beat of his heart flutter into my own because we were both brave enough to write things on those pages that shyness might have prevented us from saying.

Daughter, I have kept those precious letters. They will be a legacy to you. Someday you might read them and our story will give you comfort. You'll read about the young woman who wore a red raincoat her sister (your Aunt Anne) sent her all the way from London. I could hardly wait to write to your father and tell him about that wonderful gift. Through reading those letters you will also open that crinkly parcel delivered by your own grandfather who was postman in that midlands town for most of his life. You will hear the sounds and scents of the bustling city Anne emigrated to so she could train and become a fine nurse. All that excitement tumbled out onto the table as the vibrant colour of that coat lit up the kitchen.

Your grandmother's worried creases soon smoothed away as she read the letter enclosed for her. All well, a Christmas visit home planned and immediately looked forward to and prepared for. Your grandmother carried it around in her apron pocket all day and as she did her rounds, checking the sockets, turning off the lights.

Daughter, you might actually be able to see the girl, now your mother who wore that coat, crossing the bridges of the town she grew up in, loving every nook and cranny of it, from the outline of the steeple of St Brendan's Church to the winding journey of the Camcor. How often I'd walked by those drifting waters under the sheltering branches of oak and willow. How I loved the drapery shops in the town also, smelling of oilcloth and linen. Those journeys were often replayed in my mind as I woke up in Dublin to hear the sounds of buses screeching by the door of the house full of bedsits, where I was so lonely for one whole year before I met your father and the light and happiness of enduring love came into my life.

Ah my darling. I see that your special someone has not texted you back now for ... oh ... ten minutes! Ten whole minutes. Daughter, it is my dearest hope that the time will come when you realise that only a letter will do to bridge whatever gap separates you from the one you love. That the message sent out in haste and without much thought, is like the message scrawled on the sands, washed away with the incoming tide. I want much more for you than that, a legacy of tangible treasures that can be read and savoured on those rainy days when the heart and soul need nourishment. When you might open the envelope as if it were a portal to a very magical place and say; 'Ah, I remember now, that day, that place, that very special someone'.

Spring Clean

My idea of housework is to sweep the room with
a glance.

– Erma Bombeck

Paula Meehan's wonderful poem 'The Pattern' (from
Mysteries of the Home) brings an abiding memory of myself
and my sisters wrapping strips of old sheets around our
stockinged feet in preparation for making circles of eight
over the lino in our kitchen and hall. The furniture was
pushed back against the walls and chairs stacked one on
one to allow for freedom of movement. Even so, the 'rink'
in our small house was not wide enough for dizzy spins or
too much fancy footwork. However the smell from a large
tin of Mansion House Polish filtered through the rooms a
beautiful lavender scent that lasted for days. The same
smell issued from the open windows of all the houses
down our row.

As soon as bright golden daffodils began to appear the
women in my street were imbued with a desire to
overhaul the houses and to enjoy a good spring clean. The
constraints of squally weather meant that winter
clotheslines only bore the absolute necessary. Now that
bright sunshine and gentle winds crept into the yards the
washboards were extra busy. Heavy blankets and curtains
were given the carbolic treatment, a soap that took no
quarter when it came to cleanliness. Its vivid colour and its

strong odour was a stalwart of both scullery and Belfast sink.

Windows stripped of net curtains were, in the case of my own childhood home, sectioned into panes, dividing our back garden into small square glimpses, like photographs, of galvanised shed rooftop and small vegetable patch. Nowadays allotments are very popular but back then, in the late 1960s, every neighbour in the street grew their own supply of vegetables. Carrots and cabbages were fresh for the table, along with potatoes and leeks.

We washed the windows with Fairy liquid suds and then shone them to a dazzling brightness with old newspapers kept especially for the purpose. Elbow grease synchronised to the sound of showbands on the radio kept us all in motion. Many's the dull veneer of a sideboard was dusted to the rhythm of Brendan Bowyer belting out a popular song, or the sound of The Clipper Carlton or The Capital. This was before electric guitars and synthesizers so the superstar bands of the day usually had a very voluble brass section. But if the bands had their brass, so too the fireplace. The shining up of a jaded-looking fender seemed to take ages but was very worthwhile when its true beauty emerged once more and we could see our reflections in it. The black leading of the range was another matter and left us looking like coal miners until mother produced hot soapy water and a big smile of encouragement for all our work. Each one of us was given a specific duty according to age and size. These duties could range from 'salting the cups' (great for removing tea stains) to scouring the saucepans with a wiry pot scrub. Whoever got the task of 'running to the shop' for a necessary cleaning item that might be in short supply was deemed the lucky one. Having the chance to go out into the town meant an opportunity to meet up with friends.

More often than not a piece of news was also brought back with the shopping bag and that kept our tongues as well as our hands busy.

Removing the Miss Havisham size cobwebs from the ceiling meant standing on a rickety chair and holding aloft a duster which was really an old towel wrapped around the broom handle. Safety depended on a sibling holding the chair steady, but if there was a giddiness in the air, again thanks to a lively tune on the radio, the webs were sometimes left in place while a jive around the room dusted off our own winter blues. When ironing the sheets and shirt collars of our father and brothers, we used starch to get that crisp, new look. Our reward for such careful diligence appeared in cone-shaped bundles of boiled sweets bought in the shop perched on the bridge at the bottom of the hill where we lived. At the end of a week's hard work when everything in the house, from a yellowing spoon to a faded-looking pair of curtains, was revived again, we were treated to a visit to that shop and could have our pick from the large steel tins that lined the shelves. The shopkeeper, a lovely jolly woman, kept the cans turned on their sides so the colours and the scents could be enjoyed. Bonbons looked as if they'd been dipped in powder, clove drops were creamy shells with a red fiery centre. Other favourites included Peggie's Leg, Barley Sugar, Bulls' Eyes, Acid Drops, Butterscotch and Pear Drops. The chocolate centres of some of the boiled sweets melted like velvet, an extra treat when the outer casing was gone. The sweets were weighed on a scale, according to the available spend, and then scooped into waxy paper bags or twisted into a paper cone.

FLOUR

We should consider every day lost on which we
have not danced at least once.

                       – Friedrich Nietzsche

My mother is beginning to dance. Her steps falter at first
before finding their rhythm. At least this small, round-
bellied woman in a floral apron stained with flour looks
like my mother. She has the same short, brownish-
coloured hair clipped to the side and eyes the same shade
of blue. The kitchen is as normal too. A small space, filled
with the awkward presence of a sideboard with a dull
shine, a dresser painted green and on it a mix of crockery.
Cracked plates and tiny china cups with rose-patterned
centres. Big mugs with navy stripes. Nothing belonging to
a full set. Although it's early June, the May altar is still in
place beneath the rows of mismatched crockery, with a
bowl of wild cowslips placed before a chipped statue of
Our Lady. Her blue cloak shows some of the milk-white
chalky substance she's made of and one of her fingers is
missing. Sometimes mother says the statue is like a
crumbling cliff. Mother came from Galway, a place of
ocean and seagulls, but now she's in the midlands with
nothing but brown bog and flat landscape. One day, after a
row that shook the doors on their hinges and scattered us
like birdseed out into the yard, I heard her say she cursed
she ever came here to this town.

My mother and the man she is dancing with stumble a little as they make the turn at a sharp corner of the kitchen table. He pulls her to him and laughs, throwing back his head like the horse in Hoare's field at the end of the lane behind our house. I half expect to see steam coming out of his mouth as if it is cold October and not early summer. The cowslips placed in a rinsed out jam-jar on the dresser grow in a madness of butter yellow in those same fields behind our council house in a street perched on a hill. When I was much younger I was so very glad our house was set well back from the top of the hill and not one of the houses slanting down its angle.

The music the dancers cannot resist is not the céilí music mother usually has on. She loves the Kilfenora Céilí Band and all the better to hear their insistent, pounding beat she raises the volume on the radio whenever they come on. If she's at the table making bread or at the sink washing clothes, she'll shape the dough and pummel old work-shirts and dresses with great energy. 'Dancing with her hands' she calls it. The Kilfenora's brass and reed sound seems to suit our kitchen better than the cadences of this slow waltz which brings the creamy taste of chocolate to my mouth. But the dancers are as one with it, they could be dancing in infinite space, without obstacles, so smoothly they avoid the furniture. Even the Stanley range, sitting some way out from the wall, doesn't cause them any trouble. A black range or 'the monster' as mother calls it. Sometimes she curses its stubbornness, trying to light it each morning with newspapers dipped in white spirit. The smell of the spirit lasts for ages after but it soon catches with the briquettes and roars up the chimney. It's like looking into hell, as the nun describes it at school. There's always white spirit in the house because of the regular outbreaks of head-lice. Mother checks our hair regularly. Over the only source of heat in the house, a shelf juts out like a metal promontory. It's usually full of clothes airing.

But today it's empty of school uniforms, socks or tea-towels because it's Sunday. Already we've been to church and sat in the balcony looking down at our neighbours, at their bright scarves and shiny bald heads.

Above this metal shelf a mirror hangs, suspended on twine doubled up for strength. When we want to see ourselves we must stand on a chair and then bend our heads so that we are always craning into it, our faces becoming flushed from the heat of the range. On either side of this claw-footed monster are two armchairs, scented and beaten out of shape by the children of the house, the five who are still living at home. Our eldest sister has gone to work in Dublin in the civil service. She comes home some weekends, perfumed and lipsticked, with seams in her stockings and black shiny shoes with narrow pointed toes and high heels. She smells of hair lacquer and cigarettes. Mother warns her to be careful with her stilettos on the lino, not to pierce holes in it. This particular afternoon the youngest of the tribe, me at thirteen, sits on top of squashed cushions raised even higher by a pile of old newspapers. It's the chair nearest the one tiny window, now lit by a strong afternoon sun. The window is dressed halfway up from the sill with a net curtain and sectioned into squares of glass panes, each one presenting a photograph of galvanised rooftop, wooden fence, chickens in a wire coop.

But here, before my eyes, my mother and the man she is dancing with are finding enough room to glide and dip, bend and swirl. Her teeth gleam between her pink lips, teeth that are Ajax powder white. New teeth, they were fitted the same day as her old ones were taken out. That day, months ago, seemed endless to us. We were not used to her being away from the house and didn't know what to do with ourselves. We swept the floor and made the beds and peeled the vegetables for our dinner. We knew that her teeth gave her lots of pain and she often used pepper to try and ease it, or took tablets bought in the chemist shop we rarely visited. Come evening time we watched for her bicycle to come over the hill and ran to her when she alighted. She looked tired and her face seemed different, distorted. When she smiled that first shocking smile I felt I was looking at a stranger, but her eyes were the same bright blue. Her hands are now very white also, sprinkled with the flour that was sieved into the bowl half an hour earlier.

The Strauss waltzing tune plays on. Walnut encased, the radio sits on the sideboard. Sometimes the radio hisses its humours. It has to be tuned in and my father curses because he wants to get the racing results from Epsom or Chepstow and when the radio won't oblige, I have to run down the road with the rolled-up newspaper and the stub of a pencil to Jack the Cobbler whose kitchen has no lino and where he mends shoes on an iron last. Jack's face is always black. He uses coal, not briquettes and the smell of soot can be inhaled almost from the garden gate. But today the music is like silk, not a crackle, nothing but clear notes, old time, one, two, three, one, two.

I turn my face towards the chickens outside the window. When they first came here, I'd known them as soft yellow balls of fur. Now their skinny legs and bodies are lengthening their shadows on the hard ground, covered in lank feathers. Each spring, a new batch comes into the top square of the town on the bus, encased in large cardboard boxes. Myself and my mother collect them together, carrying home one air-holed box between us. We carry the box down through the town, over the bridge and up the hill I think is so steep, especially at Christmas time when frost coats it and makes it treacherous. Then, father grumbles about falling from his bicycle delivering the post. During this season of ice he dips a poker in the range and when it's roaring red he runs it along the rubber soles of his shoes to make them grip better. The smell fills the house and catches in our throats. All the way down the town the chicks cheep loudly and sometimes dart their tiny beaks from the airholes. Placed beside the range for a short while I love to hold them and stroke their soft yellow fluff.

But the weeks have gone by and now the chicks are no more. I dislike their shape-shifting bodies and hate it when one appears on the table for our meal. Imagining what happens to them, the twisting of their long necks, is far fiercer than witnessing my mother actually doing it. I close my eyes, shaking away the squawk of fowl while a waltzing tune lazes out from the radio. As if it now conspires to turn the kitchen into a half dream of a woman dancing with a man who is not my father. A man with his hair slicked back with Brylcreem for Mass earlier on. A man who has exchanged his Sunday shirt and navy suit for a navy blue jumper, old weather-beaten shoes, gardening corduroys and who has come in from digging with fresh vegetables for our dinner.

Earth caked on carrots and cabbages have been shaken vigorously onto newspapers. The orange of the carrots glimmer like lanterns through the dark clay, and cabbages, green and moist, keep their sweet white hearts hidden under swirls of leaf. This man who during the week sometimes comes home late from town with a brooding face is now smiling down into the face of the woman he holds in his arms.

My face burns as I watch this pied piper place his arms around my mother's waist. He looks down into her face as they spin around the kitchen table littered with the mixing bowl and apples cored and peeled, wheeling like birds at the edge of a cliff. It's happened so unexpectedly that there's no time to hesitate, my mother leaning into the music, forgetting time and place, and the youngest of her brood watching from her perch on the faded cushions of an armchair in the corner of the kitchen. I wish my brothers were here and not at football in the playing field at the farther end of the town. My mother's hands on his shoulder leave a white stain, the print of her fingers clearly visible. It's like the chalk we use in the schoolroom, the blackboard a maze of figures or Irish phrases we must learn by heart.

I look at my mother's legs and feet. She wears thick stockings because she has veins and she wears check-patterned slippers, bright red alternating with green. She's had them since Christmas and says she could walk to Gort in them they are that comfortable.

Two sets of feet slide together in perfect time. The smell of baking fills my nostrils, the pies made just before he came in from the garden, the apples bursting through the pastry, sugar and cloves mingle in a scent that drifts out of the monster's metal door. I close my eyes and dissolve into the scent and the music of a slow waltz, until my mother is wearing white gloves and the violet satin evening gown I saw in Harrington's Drapery window a few weeks before. Miles of gleaming floor tiles are reflected in mirrored walls and chandeliers. Perfume wafts its heady fragrance from my mother's soft hair and the man at her elbow whispers something that makes her turn her face away and laugh.

Someday I will go to hear the showbands at the local hall with my older sister. I will dress up as she does in bright net-lined dirndl dresses bought in the big department stores on O'Connell Street or Henry Street. I too will spray lacquer on my hair and wear high heels. I'll rouge my pale cheeks and slick bright lipstick over my pale mouth. Father calls it war-paint but mother stands behind my sister at the dressing table mirror and helps her backcomb her hair into place. They look dreamy as they both stare into the mirror that has an oval shape and is painted yellow to match the curtains.

But the big pot with our dinner in it begins to boil and the sound of bubbling water rises over the music's deepening crescendo. The white gloves fade down the lengthening shadow of a long corridor and once again, I see the mark of my mother's hands on the shoulder of this man she is dancing with in the middle of the afternoon. This man who is surely not my father. My father normally sleeps most afternoons as he works the night shift in the local telephone exchange. Then, my brothers and I have to creep around the house when we come in from school and not make a sound in case we wake him. I sometimes think how odd it is that he should be connecting up so many conversations around the town when he is so silent himself. I think of the switchboard and all those wires coming out of it like a Medusa's head. That's how he has explained it to me. A Medusa with a throng of rubber wires and a metal switchboard that on a busy night is constantly lighting up so that he can't even have a quick snooze in case the doctor or a nurse is needed or an ambulance sent for in the nearest town.

Some of the flour shakes onto the lino. Barely perceptible, a thin line of powder which will be swept up and placed in the range with the rest of the sweepings. The music twirls the dancers faster and faster around the swelling spaces in this kitchen. My heart quickens also, afraid they will both come crashing down. This man who is surely not my father grips my mother tighter to him as the last notes take them to the last dizzying spin. Then, she looks up at his face as if she is waking from a trance. He scratches his temple in a shy gesture but the smile stays on their mouths as the room contracts and the world teeters on its axis before steadying once more.

THE SHOE CAVE

> I met in the street a very poor young man who was
> in love. His hat was old, his coat worn, his cloak was
> out at the elbows, the water passed through his
> shoes, – and the stars through his soul.
>
> – Victor Hugo

Roger Vivier invented the stiletto heel in 1954, two years
before I was born. His magnificent shoes have graced the
feet of luminaries worldwide. Coronations and first
performances were the order of the day for this gifted
designer who once made a pair of boots for Rudolf
Nureyev. As I looked at the glossy pictures of Vivier's
creations, gorgeous velvet and satin concoctions, I thought
of how my mother once kept a shoe press on one side of
the fireplace stuffed full of all our discarded footwear. She
collected them as if they were the crown jewels and spoke
of them in that regard. They were security, she would say,
for the rainy day when we might not have the money for a
new pair.

We christened it the shoe cave and every time it was
opened out would tumble the old reliables that had seen
us through summers or winters. They had long lost their
shine but waited faithfully to be called back to service.
Each pair had its own story and was also stamped with the
personality of the wearer. My sandals took the worst
blackguarding, as mother called it, from all that shinnying

up concrete to walk the high wire of thin strips of walls behind the houses. I'd imagine I was part of some famous circus act, even though all I had for an audience was a field full of cows, and for a safety net, a clump of stinging nettles. One of my sisters had bunions and so her shoes bubbled out at the sides. Mother had corns and would make an appropriate incision in the leather and use these revamped shoes as slippers in the house. They were a source of great comfort to her, especially if she was 'breaking-in' a new pair. When she'd come back from shopping or visiting friends, she'd collapse into them, vowing never to part with them and woe betide anyone who'd even contemplate such a move in a fit of spring cleaning.

Both my brothers played football. Their boots were testimony to matches played on soggy ground and they nearly had half the field embedded in them. We joked about that and said we'd have mushrooms for sure the next time we'd open the shoe press. My father's shoes were size twelves. Sometimes we'd clomp around in them, slapping up and down the hallway while our parents held their breath in case we broke our necks. Father was a postman whose transport was the bicycle. He hated the winter and the slippery footpaths it brought. Often, father would have his shoes repaired to get the maximum value from them and one of us would run down to Jack at the bottom of the street. Jack was as handy as a small pot with the last. He'd always have the front door ajar and the smell of leather and polish would rush out to meet you. Row upon row of shoes looked at the world from unlaced eyelets. Communication was kept to a minimum because Jack would be listening out for racing results on the crackling radio he was continually tuned to.

When my sisters started to go dancing, the stilettos came along. They weren't Roger Vivier's, but they were slimline enough to make these young women look tall and elegant. Mother feared for the lino as the dagger-shaped heels threatened to pierce through to the concrete floor. I don't know how they danced in them, but they did.

It was platforms for me in the late seventies and the first time I wore them I felt as if I was walking on stilts. I had an aerial view of the world. Bright yellow they were, with a blue stripe, like some exotic bird. When their day was done, they met the same fate as their predecessors. For years, all these shoes jostled for space in mother's shoe press. Although our baby shoes turned yellow, mother held onto them. She also kept the black boots I wore when I sang 'The Boston Burgler' during a 'fit-up' show that came to town one winter. Eventually, we did clear out the shoe press, but not before reliving all those miles of road that we had travelled together as a family.

Fine Feathers and Beauty Queens

> Women's modesty generally increases with their beauty.
> — Friedrich Nietzsche

That particular day I'd been knee-deep in feathers plucking turkeys in an alleyway in the main street of the town. Christmas 1972 was approaching, so myself and my brother were making some extra money for the festive season.

We were sturdy youngsters, well wrapped up for the seasonal chill. I was sixteen and my brother nearly eighteen. With feathers flying around us, we must have resembled figures in a snow dome. Some of our pals would run towards us at intervals, as if bush beating, making turkey gobbling sounds for the gas of it.

The laughter kept us warm as the afternoon stretched towards early evening. We were like uilleann pipers wrestling the necks and the limbs of the hapless birds into the most comfortable position. The only 'music' however was the scraping sound of plucking quill from bone. Our hands, after a few hours, were blue but we were going to a dance that night in a parish hall a few miles out the road. We had a lift there with a neighbour.

A bowl of stew and a good wash later we prepared for our arrival at the venue. When we got there, in my innocence, I thought the hall was rigged out like fairyland. There were lanterns and balloons strung around the ceiling. As a result, a heavy mauvish shade deepened the already burning heat in the faces of the dancers.

I had borrowed a dress from a pal who had just gotten a parcel from England so I was the height of fashion. The dress had been bought down the markets in Shepherd's Bush but to me, it was as glamorous as an Yves Saint Laurent original. I had also borrowed my pal's Roman sandals, contraptions that were laced up along the leg to the knee. The band was in full swing, céilí dancing being popular and great to rise the blood. There was nothing like the 'Walls of Limerick' to bring inhibitions tumbling down. For me there would be no such thing as standing shyly on the sidelines. I couldn't wait to get out and dance and I made full use of my brother as a partner instead of waiting around to be asked onto the floor.

There was extra excitement in the air because a competition was being held to crown 'Miss Mod 1972'. The rivalry among some of the women was fierce as a result. My mother refused to allow me wear too much 'powder and paint' so I was quite bare-faced compared with the amount of rouge and lipstick in evidence. I thought the make-up on the other young women was gorgeous however and I wouldn't have minded my hair being lifted an inch or two with lacquer. Still after a day plucking turkeys and sitting in a cold alleyway, dancing was all I wanted.

Some of the young women there had plucked alongside me earlier that day, but they remained like waxworks by the wall with the effort of keeping their make-up intact. Anyone would think it was the Miss World that was being decided!

A ticket with a number was thrust into my hand by one of the adjudicators doing the rounds of the hall. He looked me over as if I was a prize heifer. I suppose he didn't know what to make of the spectacle before him. My cheeks were like hot coals from all the exertions and, not having any lacquer in my hair, meant it was flying around my face in all directions.

The straps of my Roman sandals kept slipping down my legs, resembling Nora Batty's stockings in *The Last of the Summer Wine*. At the end of the night, I was wild-eyed and dishevelled. But to give truth to the saying 'fine feathers don't always make fine birds', wasn't it my number that was called by the adjudicator. I was brought up onto the stage and handed a large box of Cadbury chocolates. Conscious of envious eyes upon me, I reckoned that if there'd been some of those feathers from earlier on going and a bit of tar I'd have been run out of town.

My brother was delighted, looking forward to an unexpected chocolate beanfeast which the whole family enjoyed around the fire on Christmas Day. The Cadbury box-lid was used as a decoration for the small grate in the parlour until eventually, many years later, the big purple bow and the two kittens on the front began to show their age. A bit like myself nowadays, I suppose. Still , when I think back to that Christmas night when I was crowned 'Miss Mod', some of the vigour of the young girl that I was then feathers around me like swirls of dancing snow.

GARDEN PARTY AT ÁRAS AN UACHTARÁIN

The homes I like the best are totally occupied, busy, and useful, whether it's a tiny little house or a great big one.

– Martha Stewart

Summer time is the season for balmy sun-filled days, long relaxing evenings and seaside picnics. It's also the time of year when Áras An Uachtaráin opens its doors for garden parties, generously giving members of the public a day out they will never forget. In the company of a writers' group I'm a member of, Platform One from Tallaght, I was lucky enough to attend a garden party at the Áras, one of the eight held annually which attracts various organisations from all corners of the country. Going up the avenue lined with oak trees planted by visiting dignitaries, I couldn't wait to get my first glimpse of the house, a building which fortunately was saved from demolition by the outbreak of World War II. The front of the house boasts an intricate centrepiece in the shape of a harp.

Excitement was palpable as I waited in the impressively handsome Francini Corridor, lined with busts of previous presidents, an office in existence since 1937 when Douglas Hyde became the first President of Ireland. A large portrait of Maud Gonne continually drew my eye, the beauty that captivated William Butler Yeats for most of his life. Although the queue was long, good humour was everywhere in evidence and who wouldn't be in great form, looking out the large windows at exquisitely-manicured grounds, splashed with bright colours from roses, geraniums and campanulas, gloriously in bloom. The meet and greet with the present incumbents of such an architectural feast, designed by Nathaniel Clements in the mid-eighteenth century, was the first event of the day. Having walked along the thickly-carpeted corridor, admiring the bronze faces of previous presidents (which included Mary McAleese and Mary Robinson), it was indeed a pleasure to be in the presence of this very popular couple. They both exude such positive energy and charm.

Once outside on the lawns, the sun continued to shine (the day of our July visit was one of the hottest of the year so far, though not quite as hot as the 33 degrees recorded on 26 June 1887). The lawns, with not a blade of grass out of place, are dominated by a giant redwood tree planted by Queen Victoria in the mid-nineteenth century.

Also in evidence, thanks to the National Transport Museum, is the open-topped tram which survived the Easter Rising and the 1913 Lock Out. The sultry voice of Galway singer Mary Coughlan was coming from a large marquee filled with seats for the musical entertainment to follow, once we had been treated to a feast of delicious food in an adjacent building. No matter what the delights of a cool drink (also on offer in the marquee), there's just nothing to beat that cup of tea. Sipping from china stamped with the distinctive harp (also present on the navy-coloured napkins), it was very relaxing to sit and enjoy sandwiches and tiny scones with jam and cream. The jam no doubt was made from the many organic fruit trees nearby (raspberry, strawberry, plum, apple, pear). There are no artificial fertilisers used. Under the care of head gardener, Robert Norris, the walled gardens, fragrant with herbs and vegetables, have been divided into four sections, each representing a season. A nest of blue tits located there in 1910 was the subject of Derek Mooney's 'NestWatch' until the fledglings left for the wider world.

Having eaten and drunk our fill, our happy band headed back to the marquee to sample entertainment provided by Ireland's leading entertainers. The rousing set by the Tulla Céilí Band reminded us just why this band is still around since its formation in 1946. The selection of reels played raised the roof. Every garden party is different but one thing is sure, every taste in music is catered for. As well as the distinctive jazz-laden voice of Mary Coughlan and the feisty traditional rhythms of the Tulla Céilí Band, The Walls and Key West Bands provided the younger folk with an invigorating rock programme.

There's a saying that goes something like: 'The man who made time made plenty of it'. Unfortunately, I certainly didn't find that to be the case at the Áras. So enjoyable was the whole event that the day sped by and before we knew it, President Higgins took to the stage to give a gracious speech thanking us for coming along. Tours of the house were on offer to round off the day before the buses began arriving to drop people to convenient pick-up destinations at Heuston Station and nearby Ratra House. If only every day was an Áras day, I couldn't help thinking as we left. However, it's good to know that our heritage is in such good hands as President Higgins and his wife Sabina, who as it happened, were celebrating their 39th wedding anniversary on that particular day in July 2013.

An Exile from Birr

> Happiness is not only a hope, but also in some
> strange manner a memory ... we are all kings in
> exile.
>
> – G.K. Chesterton, *The Thing*

In Clonmel in the early 1990s I attended a talk on writing
by one of our best-loved authors, Benedict Kiely, who
sadly is no longer with us. I bought his book, *Land without
Stars* and before he signed it for me, he asked where I was
from. My midlands accent back then was rather
pronounced – and it still is for that matter. I explained that
I was living in Tallaght since the late 1970s and had put
down roots there. In consequence of that, Benedict Kiely
signed my book, 'For an exile from Birr ...' an inscription
I've often revisited over the years.

Even after all this time, Christmas is still cause for
taking stock. More than any other season, the whole
concept of 'home' – hearth and heart – rises to the surface
like a silvery fish wanting to explore the riverbank. I came
to Tallaght New Town (as it was called then) at the foot of
the Dublin Mountains as a young bride with a lovely new
husband and a new baby son. We had very little in the
way of material possessions and there were very few
facilities, quite unlike the commercial and cultural
metropolis now in existence. Indeed, when I look at our
skyscrapers, tier upon tier of twinkling lights rising almost

as high as the mountains, I realise with a little shock how much the landscape has changed.

The valley of Glenasmole is still there, with all the beauty of its flora and fauna and the mythical legends associated with Oisín's return from Tir na nÓg to the mountains are still alive and well. Now, however, our community is a multicultural and multifaceted one with all its associated rewards and challenges.

In 1986, however, I suppose I was more than a bit of an exile. I was living in a new house in a new housing estate, with two growing boys. I was lonely as I had no close relatives living near. I was also working on the night-pack in a local supermarket, trying to save as much money as possible with Christmas approaching. I worked with a team of other ladies (wonderful women all, I bless their good humour for easing away the tiredness on those late shifts). We packed the supermarket shelves when the store closed, so on late night opening we were often there until 2.00am.

At Christmas time we packed rows and rows of candied peel, packets of sultanas, raisins and currants, dried almonds, brown sugar, flour, spices and all the other ingredients which were whipped off the shelves again the next day. To the backing track of Bing Crosby singing 'White Christmas', and all the other seasonal favourites, we were responsible for making sure that all the seasonal fare in this Christmas bazaar was topped up on a nightly basis. Our anxiety rating must have hit the roof at times, each item reminding us of all we still had to do in terms of our own baking and cleaning. We had a bus laid on each night to take us home due to the lateness of the hour. There were no skyscrapers then, hiding stars or shielding a moon shining like a glacé cherry. We sang our way home through estates with newly-planted trees, oak, alder and fir, careful not to omit a chorus of 'Liverpool Lou' for our lass from Liverpool who went back there every Christmas with her family, no matter what the cost.

As my own family had swelled to two little boys, it was no longer feasible to make the journey to the midlands for Christmas Day. We were getting used to spending the big day in Dublin but I missed the midlands as my own memories of childhood and the excitement attached to the joys and wonders of such an occasion were still steeped in the Georgian town of Birr, situated on the river Camcor, a tributary of the little Brosna. St Brendan founded a monastery there in the sixth century and gave his name to the church where I made my First Holy Communion and Confirmation and where I went every Sunday to Mass with my parents and my brothers and sisters. I had not yet formed such a 'history' with my new home in Dublin. I missed the huckster shops and drapery stores where every purchase was wrapped in the tinsel of laughter and hearty conversation.

Thirty years later, I am the mother of four children (two grown men and two girls, eighteen and thirteen respectively) and also I am a grandmother. What do Benedict Kiely's words mean to me now? Am I still an exile? And what does 'going home' for Christmas really mean? For me, it is surely about having my children around me, even if the 'tall' buildings sometime transform the skyline into a *Land without Stars*. After all these years, we have written our own history on an ever-changing landscape, along with all the other pioneering families who came here with us.

FROM THE ROYAL SCHOOL

It's now a week since I saw the boy King Tutankhamun
put on show in Dublin. Taken from his resting place
inside three coffins – which in turn were housed in four
containers leafed in golden hieroglyphics. Replicas all,

as if the past might be constructed from old photographs
and settled under glass. Left in total darkness.
Absolute stillness. Until layers unpeel beyond a golden
mask. Under that again, wrapped in linen shrouds
eyes, ears, nose and mouth.
Here in Armagh, I'm bound to be reminded
and by the smallest thing no less, a clump of petals,
withering on the path outside this door
fallen out of bouquet or hanging basket – like a yellow
chick from its nest – who cares or who can tell?
Yet bringing me love notes all the same,
strewn by a child bride before the lid was closed.

In the Royal School, that first night's sleep tears
on the briars of finding peace in a strange place.
Still ... I wake to Harold's Cross, hear traffic rumbling by.
Headed towards the city of my eighteenth year.

A narrow, single bed
takes me to the present tense, reaching for ghost warmth;
my husband's sleeping back.

This small window tells me how little or indeed,
how much I piece together that makes sense.
A town is a town, is a town is a town.
I can pull my blind up or roll it down.

From these remnants I sew. Curving pathways
flanked by green. A wild bird, mysterious Ibis?
Or just a solitary crow pecking for an early worm
as my pen pecks at blank pages.
That bird is usurped at evening by pigeons –
roosting in McGarry's shed in the midlands
where I come from – forcing out such guttural sounds.

Across tracks of green and time, houses lean together,
gossiping in mime. Beyond those houses, a rush of angles,
streets shielding each other from full view and scarce a
glimpse of moon. Muscles in my thighs feel the steep rise
to Market Square. Armagh Cathedral. Bearings taken from
the launderette at its gates boasting 'squeaky clean' while
collapsing. Into ruin.

My window sill is wide enough to sit upon. If Lancelot
comes I will gladly gaze upon his trace.
For I've not seen one living soul pass beneath these panes,
only swallows gorging on the wing
for flying south.

The Royal School seals me in. Swaddles of stairwells.
Each one leads to another story. Across the mall are names
inscribed in stone, names I knew the childhood taste of;
Smith, Durcan, Talbot, Delaney, Walsh, Daly, Boyce,
Wilson, McNally, McCarthy and O'Neill.

These voices silenced now, this monument a meeting
place. Young men and women stake their claims to life and

love, while children play on the canon as if it were an iron
horse riding out at noon or grazing, staying put.

It's that time of year too. End of summer bricking itself up,
dresses in the shops touched by strangers are marked
down, soon-to-be covered in polythene. Put in storage.

I half expect to see my mother in Armagh. These streets
appear to be the same as home.
A town is a town is a town is a town.
Or, a neighbour long since dead,

Sarah Purcell. Her blue black hair, the one luminous thing
glinting under sunlight. A woman whose sleeves rolled to
the elbow. Who kept her legs, arms and head bare.
Breathing every bit of air.

Her house was the last one on our road to be connected,
electricity flooding into places used to flickering shadows.
Unsettling her for days. Breaking up her words in
strangest ways.

In the Beginning

I was born in the small downstairs bedroom of the council house where I grew up. The midwife Mrs Hennessy lived across the road. Almost every time I'd meet her as a child she'd say 'I delivered you'. After a while I began to feel like one of the missives my father posted through letterboxes all over the town. As the youngest of six children, however, I had a privileged position in the family. My sisters were working while I was still in school and they were very generous to the 'baby' of the house.

My father came from the section of the town near the river. He had a lot of brothers and one sister Maud, who died young from TB. I knew little about my mother except she was from Galway and carried the sound of the sea in her voice. She was small, round and jolly whereas father was tall and could be moody. There was a great tradition of singing talent in my father's family, a gift I hear today in various strands of the family and their offspring. My maiden name, Cordial, is still rare enough but there was also a branch in Kinnitty. It's reported in *The King's County Chronicle and General Post* newspaper of 1818 that a James Cordial, a farmer from Kinnitty, County Offaly was broken into one Sunday by a gang of men who abducted his daughters. Shots were fired and a ransom demanded. Fortunately, none of the girls were harmed.

I grew up in a street where everyone knew each other. Walking down the road from my end of terrace house was sometimes an ordeal. Men were mostly stood at their front doors, smoking un-tipped cigarettes. The day was long to fill when there was no prospect of work. Gardens, though tiny, were almost botanical in their lushness, compensation no doubt for the lack of 'style' indoors. Women were always giving each other snips of this or cuttings of that and if anyone went anywhere they brought back frail shoots which would be ages trying to root in jam jars or milk bottles on windowsills.

Whenever I passed down that street, I'd look straight ahead or up to telegraph pole wires which were full of starlings strung across like calligraphy symbols. Sometimes too they reminded me of the notes in music books the nuns kept open on the piano in the convent school for students who could afford lessons. These birds made a buzzing sound like bees, there was so many of them. Above them, the chimney pots spouted smoke all year round. The sky above the chimney pots seemed to be full of clouds. A woman in a nearby street was always looking upward, her eyes tilted away from everyone. One day she walked out her front door leaving behind a husband and small children. Some years later, she returned and her husband took her back. She still looks up at the sky although I never found out where she was all those years. It's remarkable to me that her husband took her back as if she had just stepped out like the man in Derek Mahon's poem 'Antarctica', just 'for a while'.

Grandmother

The memory begins with a long woman in a bed under a window. Her silver hair has been combed into two thick plaits, her nose is beak-like, her shoulders bony under her white gown. The sheet is white too, folded over the coverlet, neatly tucked under the sides of the bed like an envelope.

It's my first Holy Communion Day. My brother, two years older than me, wears a grey jacket with his first pair of long trousers. My older sister bought my dress, puffed out from the waist and brought it from Dublin where she works in the civil service. I have white shoes, white gloves and my white bag has a single half crown in it, shiny as the medal pinned to my dress. The three of us have walked down the row of council houses, down the hill and over the bridge where two elderly ladies live, who are always covered in coal dust. We didn't stop to gaze into their sweet shop window and we wouldn't dream of going in there today anyway for fear the black powder would contaminate our new clothes. Even the frothy waters of the Camcor River couldn't tempt us to linger. We moved through the town, turned left or right at laneways and narrow streets. We passed the cinema where my sister would take us to later, until we eventually came to this street near the ruins of the workhouse.

It's a day in the month of May. Our mother is at home, either sewing, baking or working in the garden. Everyone says she has green fingers. Our house is full of begonias and geraniums, their smell is like damp earth. I don't remember much of the Communion service, except for the receiving of the Host and the fear that it might stick to the roof of my mouth.

My brother asks my sister for a drag of her cigarette and she gives it to him. He inhales deeply, getting used to the nicotine. This is not his first time to take a 'pull'. I move away from them, not wanting the smell to settle on my veil or dress. We are going to see my paternal grandmother. She's asked to see us, has written a note to my mother that was posted and delivered by my father. My middle name, Elizabeth, is the same as hers.

Her garden is gated and has iron railings around it. There are no hedges or fuchsia bushes like we have at home. Everything is covered in concrete. From the chimney a scud of smoke streaks upwards, evidence of the small fire in the grate near her bed, the only source of heat. Although warm enough outside, it's obvious this room is always chilly. We are let in by one of our uncles, a tall, thin, balding man. He comes to our house sometimes and we listen to recordings of him singing John McCormack songs. He is still unsure of our names. He moves to stir the briquettes in the grate and they break open, collapsing into themselves.

Our grandmother has both her arms by her sides, the palms facing upwards like the martyred figure of the Christ on the Cross seen earlier in the church. She peers at us, scrunching up her eyes and her face settles into a frown. She is not as I imagined. I had given her a soft, round face, framed with cotton wool soft hair. She is supposed to be sitting in a chair by the fire with her arms outstretched, ready to hug us and kiss our foreheads before peering into our faces and tracing the likeness to herself and our father in the shape of our features. I had fantasised that her kitchen would be lit with a great luminous light and the table set with big round plates and glittering cutlery.

Instead, there is nothing on the table but a chequered cloth and a glass condiment set, the salt and pepper crusted around the lid. There are no photographs on the walls, nothing but a large Sacred Heart framed in heavy wood. There are no photographs of aunts or uncles, nothing of our grandfather. All we know about him is that he helped to build the beautiful building that is the post office. We are not asked about our mother. Nothing but disapproval and unease registers in that tiny, spare kitchen. We stay for less than half an hour.

She died not long after, on Christmas day as it happened. It was a particularly cold winter when a lot of snow fell. It seemed right somehow that she should be buried when the world was white and the earth hard and unyielding.

Black is the New White

When I was a teenager, I wanted to be black. I prayed that by some miracle I would wake up some morning and be black. It would be a simple solution to a very serious problem I had, one that brought me out in hot sweats and sent me into dizzy spins of fear. The minute anyone looked in my direction, my face turned crimson, like a jar filling up with raspberry jam. My face was the same colour as the roaring red tomatoes mother dipped in sugar in the summer time on the rare occasions we had salad.

Mother was absolutely adamant that we would get an education so instead of going into Dubarry's or the Moquette, the two factories in the town at that time, we stayed on in school. An older sister did extremely well in her Leaving Certificate which earned her a scholarship. All my sisters got scholarships as they progressed in their education. When it was my turn all those support systems were gone but by then my sisters were working and often sent me parcels from Dublin and England (where one sister went to train as a nurse). Meanwhile, I was trying to make friends with girls from other areas of the town, girls who brought friends home to tea, something that I couldn't do. Our house was a two-up, two-down and the 'parlour', the little room in the hall, had to be converted to a bedroom. There was no place to sit and listen to records, to play Horslips, my favourite band then. I became friends with a few girls that I stayed friends with all through secondary school. One of them had a big house with two sitting rooms. We went there in the evenings and it was just heaven to sit in that place with high ceilings, heavy curtains and a big open fire. She dimmed the lights and in semi-darkness we listened to Cat Stevens, Billy Joel, Fleetwood Mac, among others. Because I knew I couldn't be seen properly, it was a reprieve from the constant blushing. We talked about boys we liked and what we'd do when we left school. At the age of 15, it seemed light years away.

One of those girls from our 'gang' died recently. Even though we had lost touch, I went down from Dublin to the town to pay my respects. The library with the high ceiling and which looked like a church, where I had spent much of my time as a child and young adult, is now a funeral parlour and that's where she was, in an open coffin. I sat with others who knew her thinking about her sixteen year old self. She told me how to kiss a boy as we sat in the cloakroom one day. She explained it as naturally as if she were threading a needle.

Earlier, on the day of her removal to the church, I'd gone to the cemetery to visit my parents' grave and saw the big gaping wound in the earth which would later receive the remains of this fun-loving, very popular woman. She is the first one of our 'gang' to cross over to the other side.

Peas

He was the only child of a neighbour and while we never had any convenience food in the house, he often got whole tins of peas for himself. They were Bachelor's Peas and nothing was ever as green. At that time they didn't have a ring pull like now so his mother would take the lid off with a can opener and give him a spoon. He liked to eat them cold and once or twice he gave me a mouthful to taste. They were divine. Cold on the tongue and juicy and so green they left a stain. Looking into the tin was like staring at a container full of marbles or the eyes of frogs squashed together in the big rusty iron trough in Hoare's field.

He was popular while the peas lasted. The lid wasn't properly taken off one day and he cut his finger on its jagged edge. Blood mingled with the pea juice. Was it an omen? He married a girl I went to school with. Sadly she died while still quite young. She came from a very large family, all girls, beautiful and delicate and so dignified they could have stepped from the pages of Jane Austen or Emily Brontë.

Circus

Summer 2013 I went to a travelling circus which had pitched tent in Banagher, County Offaly. The town is all hills and the circus, a family-run affair, was advertised by Mr Corvinni the Elder going about on stilts. He said going up Banagher Hill was much easier than coming down. How true. Just like on the swing-boats in the carnivals that came to Hoare's field every summer. But for all the Corvinni Brothers being so brilliant, standing one on one (four of them) all balanced on the back of a kitchen chair (on a table), there's nothing as exciting as going to the circus when you are young. I went everywhere then with my two brothers.

I can still see us sitting in the front row of the tent; we are bare kneed, skin scraped from climbing the rough dashed walls behind our council houses. We don't care about our war wounds, puffed up from slab toffee and blobby chunks of sugary jellies. A young girl who once lived in the town is performing for us on a raised wooden platform. But performing is not the right word. She is really only standing there, trying not to shiver in her scanty clothing. Chewing and watching her every move, we don't feel the wind whipping under tent flaps, creaking the timbers of the poles. Badly stained, the canvas smells of wet Sundays. I'm wearing a bobbled cardigan and scarf.

My brothers wear identical corduroy suits, in a colour brown like the mud splattered floor of the tent.

We stare at the conjuror's assistant, the young girl who is like a creature from another planet. Her face is so white that it is almost transparent, her lips ruby coloured. Around her throat glitters a thick necklace of jewels, all different hues, their depth of colour emphasising her blanched face. She is so thin that the necklace threatens to unbalance her. Black harem trousers hang around her bony hips, her waist is so tiny her chest seems to be caving in. Shoulders are bare, the chicken-size wings of her backbone protrude beneath the tight black bolero she wears. Hair is a cascade of candy-floss blonde, the edges wispy in the harsh electric light just above her head. She focuses on the conjuror, on his large hat and cane, stepping aside for him, a man much older who she had run off with the summer before. He made her disappear like a bundle of rabbits in his hat, I heard my mother say to our next door neighbour and now she's 'damaged goods'. At eleven years old, I have no idea what that means. Or why my mother frowns and tightens her mouth when I ask. I only know that the girl ran off with a conjuror old enough to be my father. She is seventeen years old. She looks so wispy, as if his hands could pass through her skin. The conjuror is thickset, solid, his face very red. His shirt is a pale yellow under a black jacket with shiny lapels. His trousers are shiny too and he is slightly smaller in height than she is. When he looks at her, his mouth draws back over gaps in his teeth but his voice, when it comes, is rich and deep. He is flipping the hat she has handed to him, letting us see there is nothing there. I don't know how or where the conjuror and his young assistant live outside this space. Mother did not want us to come but we begged and begged, wearing her down. She'd given us the coins for admission and enough over for sweets.

While we are here she is bent over the sewing machine in our kitchen making a dress for me because soon the inspector will come to the school to examine us in our writing and arithmetic. The material is cream with loads of poppies, flowers that grow wild in the field behind our house. The dress is almost ready except for the zip running the whole length of the back and the hem needing to be turned up. Father is in work, in the telephone exchange, plugging in long wires into the switchboard, connecting up the town through tunnels of tubing. And now, a long stream of scarves are being pulled from the conjuror's hat as it sits upright on the table before the magician. Scarves coloured like the rainbow pouring out of his hat. We clap our hands and whistle through our fingers. The conjuror steps back and his young assistant bounces forward on her tiny feet. He takes her dainty white hand and they bow together.

Filling in Time

When I was eighteen and newly arrived in Dublin to work in Coras Iompair Éireann, I plucked up the courage one evening and joined the Desmond Domnican Ballet Academy in Parnell Square. I saw an advertisement in the *Evening Herald* and thought I had nothing to do but show up and all my dreams of being a prima donna would materialise. There was no such thing as ballet in our street when I was growing up. No money for dancing shoes or ballet dresses. Buying me *Bunty* and *Judy* were the worst things mother could have done though. I was convinced that schools existed where midnight feasts from tuck boxes was the norm and every girl worth her salt was a ballerina. It was the pretty tulle dresses and swan feathers I was in love with. The ballerinas, gorgeous fairy-like women, were my idols.

I, on the other hand, was chunky and red-faced, not at all ethereal or waiflike. Desmond Domnican allowed me into his large room which had mirrors around it and high ceilings. As I came in the front hallway I heard a chorus of barking from upstairs and I heard later that he kept a number of dogs. Obviously, they didn't enjoy classical music or the sound of aspiring dancers pounding the bare floorboards. There were men and women of all ages. I remember one woman in particular, she must have been over sixty and had her dark hair scraped back from her face and wore a wide headband. She was dressed in leotards and was able to swing her leg right over the bar that ran the whole length of the room. For a few sessions I threw shapes is all I can say about it. Threw shapes and then reason caught up with me and outstripped my aspirations to be a dancer.

The next thing I joined was Weightwatchers. I went with a girl who had come from Clare to work in the same office as me in Heuston Station. After two weeks, this girl had lost almost half a stone and was ecstatic. What she failed to tell the slimming instructor was that she had come off her epilepsy tablets because they interfered with her diet regime. Just after weighing in, this poor girl had the worst epileptic fit I've ever had the misfortune to witness. Her whole body twitched with the spasms that shook her from head to foot and felled her like a sapling. Luckily, there was someone there with a bit of savvy who knew how to cope. When the poor girl came out of the seizure, she was gutted as obviously she herself was embarrassed by her condition. By mutual agreement, we never returned to Weightwatchers.

Workhouse

What's left of the building can be seen through gaps in a wall of oak trees. When those trees are in full leaf it's hard to make it out but when winter comes, bare branches leak light onto those grim stones. The roof is still solid in places and some of the windows have glass, some are like eyes with empty sockets. Floors still have original wood. Nearby, the river Camcor flows under the houses in the street my grandparents lived and where my father and his siblings grew up. In summer, his side of the road always seemed to be in shade, the row of houses always with the doors shut tight. In one of the houses further down the row the face of a woman peers out, her face frozen into a puzzled look, her eyes dark. She is always at that window, always looking out on a street that leaves her to herself.

In 1982 when there was little employment the sister closest to me in age worked in these ruins, packing sphagnum moss for export, an IDA initiative. The moss came from the bog where the skylark wheeled and sang its lonely tune. It was used for making insoles and flower arranging and travelled as far away as America. How strange it must have been to feast on reds, greens and bursts of ginger colour in such a place, with the wind howling around the gables and a low moan creaking through gaps.

My sister worked there with other young women and men. When it snowed, a flail of white sparks, as if from an anvil, splashed through some broken slates in the roof. She was married then and had two small boys. Her husband worked too but only when work was there. They had moved back from the city and lived with my mother and father. I was in the city then and saw her mostly at weekends when I came home on the train as far as Roscrea with my free travel from CIÉ. I had to bus it the rest of the way.

Tall windows look out onto brambles wrapped around each other, squeezing the juice from the berries that no-one picks, purpling down the thorny branches into the soil.

The sadness of the place went into her heart and soul, my sister often says, and when she went to America with her family to live for over twenty years, she sometimes thought about that place, of the long stairs that went up to the sleeping quarters above where they worked, full of the ghosts of children crying out to mothers and to absent fathers. How cold her hands must have been in that workhouse all those years ago. Whenever I think of her frozen flesh, I close my eyes and place her hands in fur-lined gloves. I find some small comfort in that.

Stargazer

Trust your heart if the seas catch fire, live by love
though the stars walk backward.

– E.E. Cummings

I went on a walking tour of Georgian Birr during the
summer. A strange thing to do really considering that I
was born and reared and lived there for the first eighteen
years of my life. Sometimes you need to leave and come
back again to see a place through fresh eyes.

Growing up in the town I doubt if I truly appreciated
the grand, elegant sweep that is John's Mall, the tranquil
river walks or the amount of colourful history associated
with this jewel in the midland crown. Thanks to the Crotty
Schism dating back to the 1830s, it's a place of many
churches and influences, of Methodist, Presbyterian and
Catholic persuasion. The Quakers came here too; their
burial ground is right at the top of High Street, where I
lived for the first eighteen years of my life. Naturally I was
far more interested in Horslips back then, playing hits like
'Dearg Doom' or 'Furniture' as loud as I possibly could
without our terraced council house imploding into the
next door neighbour's.

Birr Castle is an imposing structure at one end of the
town while at the other end the remains of the workhouse
hides its shameful past behind a copse of tall trees. In
between, there's the elegance of Georgian houses together

with more contemporary buildings such as boutiques and an Indian takeaway. The Georgians unfortunately never got to savour a Tandoori sizzler.

As a child I played with my brothers in Birr Castle Gardens, running wild down the long lens of avenue, my plaits and pleated skirts flying out behind me. As well as being an all year round feast for the senses, Birr Castle Gardens house the Leviathan, the 58 foot telescope invented by William Parsons, the Third Earl of Rosse, and which remained the largest in the world until 1917. We played cowboys and Indians around the bones of its huge circumference and afterwards went to the castle kitchens to buy cooking apples. These apples would be washed and peeled, revealing the shape of stars at their centre.

The walking tour of Birr also takes in Oxmantown Mall with its gorgeous row of fanlight topped front doors. The Mall was created by the Parson family so that the walk from the castle gates to the nearby Presbyterian Church would allow for a parade of grandeur to take place. Unfortunately, the Mall proved to be memorable for another, more tragic reason. It was on the corner of Oxmantown Mall that Mary Ward, microscopist, artist, astronomer and naturalist, was killed by one of the first steam engine motor cars, thus becoming the world's first motor fatality. It happened on 31 August 1869, the accident seen from the front room window of a doctor's house across the road in Emmet Street. Due to the uneven surface of the road, the engine jolted forward and in doing so Mary Ward was thrown from the vehicle and her head injured under one of the giant wheels. The two ladies who saw the accident from the vantage point of the window later gave evidence at the subsequent inquest. It seems incongruous that such an accident should take place at all, especially since the speed limit, imposed in 1865 by the

Red Flag Act, was only four miles an hour in the country and two miles an hour in the town.

It would be a shame if the circumstances of Mary Ward's death overshadowed the many talents she was gifted with. Born near Ferbane, twelve miles or so from Birr, in 1827, she came from a renowned scientific family. William Parsons, the Third Earl of Rosse, was also her first cousin and she was a regular visitor to the castle. Mary was a keen stargazer herself and so her drawings of insects would be accurate she used a magnifying glass. So great were her abilities in this regard that the astronomer James South persuaded her father to buy her a microscope. While the Third Earl was constructing the Leviathan telescope, Mary Ward made drawings at each stage which were so fine that they proved invaluable when the telescope was restored in recent times. She made her own slides from slivers of ivory as glass was scarce at the time. Mary Ward had the honour of being one of only three women on the mailing list of the Royal Astronomical Society, the other two being Queen Victoria and Mary Somerville. In 1854 she married and gave birth to eight children, a feat in itself, but she still found time to privately publish *Sketches with the Microscope* in 1857.

Because of the constraints on Victorian women she had neither access to education or libraries, yet she made the most of her opportunities. Her book triumphed when Groomsbridge Publishers in London published it under the title *The World of Wonders as Revealed by the Microscope*. So great was its popularity, it was reprinted eight times between 1858 and 1880.

I don't think I will ever walk in Birr Castle Gardens again without thinking of this talented and tenacious Victorian woman who looked to the stars for inspiration.

THE STAMP OF APPROVAL

> Letter writing is the only device for combining
> solitude with good company.
>
> – Lord Byron

When I was growing up, the question was often asked:
'Who Made the World?' The answer would invariably be
'Vesty (short for Sylvester) Cordial'. This man was a
relative of mine and a master stonemason. Indeed, the post
office in Birr is one of the magnificent buildings in the
town he can claim credit for. My father worked in that
same post office both as a night telephonist and a postman.
He delivered the early post around the town on a big black
bicycle. He wore a heavy serge overcoat with big brass
buttons and a cap with a glossy peak on it. At that time my
father worked for the Department of Posts and Telegraphs.
It wasn't until 1984 that the department divided into An
Post and Telecom Eireann.

It's no wonder that communications had a huge
influence on my life in general. From an early age I
collected stamps, gathering up my precious hoard from
envelopes donated by neighbours who had family away
from home. Letter writing was much more common then,
the expression, 'it's in the post', a familiar one.

I collected Irish stamps mostly, of course, but seeing a
foreign one was like having a mini window on the larger
world. It's always a pleasure still when a new stamp

appears. All of these mini masterpieces are a delight, right up to the 2012 Olympic stamp which is even more wonderful considering all the sporting medals Ireland received that year, Paralympics athletes included. The history of stamps is itself fascinating, ever since the famous Penny Black, the world's first adhesive postage stamp, went on sale in 1840. This was followed in 1841 by a new type of envelope which was different from the early Victorian model, folded by hand. However, by the mid 1840s, paper folding machines resulted in a standard size envelope. In 1850 the invention of a machine which allowed gummed envelopes, revolutionised stationery. In earlier times, letters were the preserve of the educated and the rich. The establishment of the national school system in the early 1800s meant that an increasing level of the population could read and write.

Over fifty years ago Dublin was at the heart of international philatelic interest. Thanks to the efforts of an Australian entrepreneur, Dr Paul Singer, Shanahan's Stamp Company was established in Dún Laoghaire in 1954. Unfortunately, a robbery in 1959 precipitated the collapse of the company.

The history of our state can be mapped by the appearance of certain stamps. The map of Ireland design, courtesy of J. Ingram, immediately points to the country's new independent status. It was issued in February 1923. In 1937 a high value definition shows St Patrick, the Apostle of Ireland, invoking a blessing on the Paschal Fire, the stamp is in a small sheet format and has no gutter margin. 1948 saw the arrival of airmail stamps designed by K.J. King. The 3d blue features the Angel Victor, the Messenger of St Patrick as he carries the voice of Ireland (Vox Hiberniae) over Lough Derg. In 1982 Irish boats, with four colour printing, marked us out as a maritime nation. This maritime themed collection was designed by Peter

Wildbur. In 2006 a Braille stamp (owing its embossed Braille design to Steve Simpson) and commemorating the 30th anniversary of the Irish Guide Dogs, was issued.

I often heard my father talking about his postmaster, a stickler for time. My father was always careful not to delay too long at garden gates engaging in neighbourly chats as a result! Imagine my surprise though when I learnt, in later years, that Sir Ernest Shackleton, the Irish explorer, was once an Irish Postmaster General? Shackleton is better recognised for the Antarctic Expedition of 1914–1917. A stamp featuring the ship Endurance and views of the Antarctic camp was designed by Ger Garland.

I have continued to collect stamps over the years. I also find that usually an appropriate stamp can be purchased to suit the occasion. With my son's wedding recently I was able to buy a lovely set of wedding stamps for posting cards and photographs to relatives. I've always considered stamps, those 3cm x 4cm, to be miniature masterpieces and the collecting of stamps not only deeply satisfying on an artistic level but also as a recorder of social history. Interestingly An Post are always open to suggestions from the public regarding design. The fact that my father was often a deliver of tidings (whether good, bad or indifferent as the saying goes) adds an extra layer of value to the enterprise. It's rarer now to see the bicycle with the wicker basket on the front trundling into the street. More likely it's the green van with the distinctive An Post emblem on the side. One thing that never changes, however, is the excitement of both sending and receiving a communication through the post, a stamp of approval that this form of contact is still very much alive and well.

FROM PARISH PUMP TO CELEBRATING
300 YEARS OF FIRE FIGHTING

I can think of no more stirring symbol of man's humanity to man than a fire engine.

– Kurt Vonnegut, *Sirens of Titan*

THE FIRE FIGHTER'S PRAYER

When I'm called to duty God
Wherever flames may rage
Give me strength to save a life
Whatever be its age.

Help me to embrace a little child
Before it is too late
Or save an older person
From the horror of that fate.

Enable me to be alert
To hear the weakest shout
And quickly and efficiently
To put the fire out.

I want to fill my calling
And to give the best in me
To guard my neighbour
And protect his property.
And if according to your will
I have to lose my life

Bless with your protecting hand
My children and my wife.
– Anon

Across the globe courageous tales of fire rescues are many and varied, even extending to the feline world in 1996 when Scarlett the cat brought her five kittens to safety from a burning Brooklyn warehouse. Fire fighters in particular, however, fearlessly risk their own lives daily in the pursuit of saving the lives of others. The sound of the fire brigade's klaxon usually brings an initial response of dread followed by prayer for the safety of all concerned. Not too long ago a fire engine was called to the urban street where I live in the middle of the night. When I looked out my window, black smoke billowed all over the houses, belched out from a burning car. The fear was that the fire would spread to nearby dwellings or that someone would be inadvertently injured through an explosion. In the event the local brigade soon quenched the flames, effectively and efficiently, reminding me of the important work they do.

Fires alas are part of every society. Every day it seems news of conflagrations are reported, more often than not accompanied by tales of bravery. Fires and their resulting devastation do not discriminate. Derelict houses are every bit as prone as the busiest apartment block complex. Fires, both large and small, are brought about by a whole range of causes. The Old Jameson Distillery in Bow Street suffered a minor fire in January 2013 due to difficulties with the air conditioning system. And who could forget the fateful night in February 1981 when the Dublin Fire Brigade were called to the Stardust dance hall in Artane? Despite the bravery of the units sent from both Kilbarrack Fire Station and North Strand, 48 people died and 214 people were injured.

While the Dublin Fire Brigade is celebrating its 150th anniversary, fire fighting in Dublin is now almost 300 years old. Ever wondered where the expression 'Parish Pump Politics' came from? In 1715 an act of parliament decreed that each Church of Ireland parish had to keep one large and one small fire engine and associated equipment. In the eighteenth century supervision of this equipment and machinery was placed under the care of a parish clerk or beadle. No training was given but there was a reward for services. Competition for this position was fierce and so, the expression 'Parish Pump Politics' arose.

Up until the installation of these all important fire engines the entire business of fire fighting was quite precarious. Dublin City had major fires in 1190 and 1283 but it wasn't until a serious fire at Saint Mary's Abbey in 1304 that the Common Council ordained there should be some system in place. Such was the destruction of the city that the Council of Dublin issued an ordinance degree which ended with 'any person answerable for the burning of a street shall be arrested, cast into the middle of the fire, or pay a fine of one hundred schillings'. By 1592 each parish had to keep six buckets and two ladders to rescue trapped parishioners. Saint Werburgh's Church on Werburgh Street boasts the oldest surviving fire fighting appliances in the city. It wasn't until 1711, however, that Dublin City purchased its first fire engines. There was no cover for out of city limits.

A fire service for all didn't come along until the Dublin Corporation Fire Brigade Act of 1862. This act was given the Royal Assent by Queen Victoria, and James Robert Ingram was appointed to organise the day to day running of the brigade. Ingram had experience of fire fighting in New York and brought an American style. With Ingram's appointment, 'The Dublin Fire Department' as it was initially known, was born. Ingram recruited 40 men, who previously worked as sailors. As a tribute to his American connection, the firemen wore red shirts while the officers wore the frock coat and kepi of the United States army. The brigade was based in two small stations with its headquarters at Coppinger Row, off South William Street and the other station was at Whitehorse yard, off Winetavern Street. The very first motor engine (R1.1090) appeared in Tara Street in 1909, though most of the brigade held onto their 'handlebar' moustaches.

Insurance companies began to filter into the Irish market in the 1720s. After the great fire of London in 1666 insurance companies began to look towards Ireland as a source of business. In 1722 the first fire insurance company was set up when the Royal Exchange Assurance (REA) had an agency in Dublin. Sun Assurance Company issued its tin fire-mark in 1810, a plate that was placed on a building to indicate it was insured.

Dublin in the nineteenth century was teeming with tenements. Fires were commonplace. James Ingram distinguished himself by his handling of two major events when he was at the helm of the brigade. A major distillery fire in the Liberties saw the streets running with burning spirits. Ingram ordered horse manure to be brought. It blocked the street and helped soak up the whiskey. Around this time also a burning ship in Kingstown Harbour was considered to be a major risk to the port. On Ingram's orders it was sunk. Ingram died from tuberculosis in 1882 and was replaced by Captain John Boyle. Despite Ingram's high profile he is buried in an unmarked grave in Mount Jerome Cemetery.

The history of the Dublin Fire Brigade, in terms of events and leadership, is a colourful one right through the ensuing decades. The First World War in 1914 saw the split into those who supported the British in the conflict and those who stayed at home and tried to win independence for Ireland. This fight kept the brigade very busy. The brigade's ambulances were a regular sight on the streets or when hospital ships returned from the front. Captain Thomas Purcell led the brigade until his retirement in 1917. Purcell oversaw the introduction of the first emergency ambulance in the city. It was used on 5 January 1898 to bring badly injured crew members from The Curlew trawler to St Patrick Dun's Hospital after an accident when a steel hawser snapped onboard. Fire fighters Tom Dunphy, Will O'Brien and Joe Kiernan were part of the team. Joe Kiernan, to this day, has descendants in the Dublin Fire Brigade. After 1956 all ambulances and engines had radios fitted. At the time of the 1916 Rising, Guinness Brewery, along with Bass and Powers Distillery, all operated functioning fire services in their establishments, due to the volume of production and the risk of fire posed. The Guinness fire fighters, along with Powers Distillery, were called upon with Pembroke and Rathmines Fire Brigades when they found themselves working against the odds. John Myers subsequently replaced Purcell to face the challenges during the War of Independence and the Civil War.

In the 1920s and 1930s, Dublin expanded and so too the city boundaries. Hard times due to a world recession were not aided by a city plagued by water shortages. The 1930s ended with the world plunged into another global war. 1941 was marked by the brigade's heroism when Dublin's North Strand was bombed by German planes. 1941 is also significant as the year of the Belfast Blitz, when hundreds of Luftwaffe aircraft dropped 200 tons of bombs on Belfast City. Although Ireland was neutral during WWII, Eamonn de Valera, then Taoiseach, decided to send firemen to help the stricken city. Volunteers went from Dublin, Dún Laoghaire, Drogheda and Dundalk. The bravery of these volunteers was largely unrecorded, until recently, due to fear of reprisals. At that time, Belfast had few air raid shelters. Also remarkable about that event is the courage of Connemara singer Delia Murphy who was singing at a concert in the Ulster Hall in the centre of Belfast when the bombing began. As the air raid warning sounded, Delia refused to leave the stage and continued her performance.

Throughout the history of the nation Dublin Fire Brigade have been heroes. Nowadays the brigade are headquartered in Townsend Street in Dublin City Centre. There are twelve full-time stations across six operational areas. Dublin Fire Brigade also have two retained stations (relying solely on volunteers) at Skerries and Balbriggan. 133,000 calls approximately are processed annually. The brigade, operating seven days a week and with a staff of approximately 900 people, are also responsible for mobilising emergency responses in areas of Leinster and Ulster. Prevention, of course, is always an ideal to strive for with regard to fires.

The Dublin Fire Brigade advocate three golden rules; the absolute necessity of having an escape drill in place, the placing of two smoke alarms (tested regularly) and also, the surveying of the home/workplace and subsequent implementation of safety measures. It's also advised not to overload electrical sockets and to avoid the build-up of paper/refuse, together with the maintaining of an adequate means of escape by keeping routes clear of all clutter.

The Dublin Fire Brigade Museum is situated at Malahide Road, Marino, Dublin 3. The museum is housed over two floors which contain a treasure trove of historical items from the brigade's history. It's also appropriate that the lives of those lost while protecting others should be commemorated. A book, *Dublin Fire Brigade and the Irish Revolution* (South Dublin Libraries) by historian and operational fire fighter, Las Fallon is now available, complete with maps, illustrations and photographs.

LINEN, WOVEN MOONLIGHT

> The amount of women in London who flirt with
> their own husbands is perfectly scandalous. It looks
> so bad. It is simply washing one's clean linen in
> public.
>
> – Oscar Wilde

There are many photographs and portraits of Jacqueline
Kennedy, a First Lady renowned not just for her beauty
but for her sense of style. It's very significant then, for her
official portrait, Jacqueline Kennedy chose to wear a full-
length gown made of pleated linen designed by Sybil
Connolly. Born in 1921 in Swansea, the designer's name
was known throughout the fashion houses of Europe and
America. By the 1960s, when the famous White House
portrait was completed by Aaron Shikler, Sybil Connolly
was an important force in the world of high fashion. Her
clothes were worn, not just by Jacqueline Kennedy, but by
the Rockefellers and the Duponts.

Sybil Connolly always promoted and used Irish tweeds
and lace but it was her designs in linen that brought the
flax fabric to prominence. She is famous for developing the
handkerchief linen, a linen so fine that it took nine yards to
make one yard of pleated material. The beauty of this
'invention' was that the fabric could be folded and packed
in such a way that it emerged unscathed, ready to wear.
No wonder it was popular with ladies who needed clothes

that lent an appearance of glamour and style, but were also durable.

In the Ulster Museum, Takabuti is preserved. A daughter of the priest of Amun who died 2,500 years ago, the linen swathed around the Mummy is still in a state of perfection. Linen, one of the earliest products known to humankind, was used extensively in the Mediterranean in pre-Christian times. Prized as a commodity it was often used as currency. The Egyptians saw the properties of linen as symbolising light and purity. They called it 'woven moonlight', wrapping their dead in linen so that their tombs might be illuminated by it.

Another name given to linen is *linum usitatissimum* which refers to the usefulness of flax itself, going back to neolithic times. At a site in Switzerland food prepared from flaxseed was found together with remnants of linen threads, ropes and fishing nets. There is no definitive date by which linen production in Ireland can be traced but myths and legends from the ninth century identify the elevated status of important men and women through their wearing of linen. By the eleventh century, flax was established as an industry and was being cultivated in Ireland to attract new settlers from England and Scotland. Although Northern Ireland became known as the Linen Homelands, the flax plant was grown in other parts of the island and big mills existed outside of Ulster. A Linen Hall was established in Clonakilty in 1820. Textile weavers also existed in the midlands until the Napoleonic wars caused a decline.

The cultivation and production of linen was very much a family affair, albeit a gruelling one in terms of labour. Men were responsible for the seeding of flax and women looked after the weeding. Flax is harvested in August, one hundred days after sowing, and grows to one metre in height. The tall stem had to be pulled with care and then bundled into sheaves (beets) before being spread into stacks called stooks and left to dry in the sun. The seeds were then removed and saved for the following year's planting or to make linseed oil or cattle feed. The next part of the process, retting, meant that the beets were placed into a pond and left to steep. The stench of decomposing plants hung heavily but this helped to separate the valuable fibres from the core of the stem. After drying came the scutching, a dusty job, beating the stems with a mallet, resulting in a tangled bunch of fine fibres. These were then straightened by a hackler using combs. The spinning of the fibres was always done by women, thus the term 'spinster'. Young children wound the yarn onto bobbins. By 1850 a third of flax spinning mills were located in the Belfast area. Women were often the only breadwinners but children as young as ten were employed in advance of them becoming full time workers at the age of thirteen. Because of the dust in the mills, workers were often susceptible to respiratory illness.

Word War II gave a boost to the linen industry as there was a high demand and also, government price controls caused the industry to flourish. The changing face of consumerism eventually saw a move away from linen. Despite high profile women like Jacqueline Kennedy's favouring of linen, cotton and easy care synthetic fibres drove the closure of two of Belfast's biggest mills at York Street and Brookfield in the 1960s.

The Irish Linen Centre and Lisburn Museum provides a comprehensive overview of Irish linen history. The centre offers a demonstration of the hand spinning of flax and handloom weaving of fine linen cloth on original looms. It's appropriate that such a facility exists in Lisburn as French Huguenot Louis Crommelin was responsible for setting up a linen factory there in 1697. The museum is situated close to rail and bus stations and provides a comprehensive insight in an exhibition entitled 'Flax to Fabric'.

CELEBRATING UILLEANN PIPES

Music is a moral law. It gives soul to the universe,
wings to the mind, flight to the imagination, and
charm and gaiety to life and to everything.

– Plato

October is the month for celebrating the uilleann pipes, not
only in Ireland but across the globe. Thanks to great Irish
musicians, such as Willie Clancy, Seamus Ennis, Liam
O'Flynn and Davy Spillane, uilleann pipes have an ever-
increasing appreciative audience. The history of the pipes
is one that speaks volumes about the tenacity of its
practitioners and their dedication in keeping the
instrument 'alive' in every sense of the word.

The first reference to bagpipes in Ireland was discovered
in an eleventh century poem 'Aonach Carman' (the fair of
Carman, found in the *Book of Leinster*). The lines were:
'Pípaí, fidlí cen gail,/Cnámfhir ocus cuslennaig,/Slúag étig
engach egair,/Béccaig ocus búridaig' ('Pipes, fiddles, men
without weapons,/bone players and pipe blowers,/a host
of embroidered, ornamented dress,/screamers and
bellowers'). Early representations of pipe playing were
found on high crosses and a rough wood carving of a
piper formerly at Woodstock Castle, County Kilkenny
dates the instrument to the sixteenth century. Although
there is no record of the pipes or any other musical
instrument being played on the field of battle in pre-

Norman Ireland, in later times the pipes were regarded as being the martial instrument of the Irish. One commentator remarked; 'To its sound this unconquered, fierce and warlike people march their armies and encourage each other to deeds and valour'. However, the pipes had a more peaceful use also. Writing in 1698 John Dunton, an English traveller, describes a wedding in Kildare thus: 'After the matrimonial ceremony was over, we had a bagpiper and blind harper that dinned us with their music, to which there was perpetual dancing'. It's true that the distinctive sound of the pipes is not to everyone's taste but when played at their best, as in the signature tune from *Titanic*, there's something plaintive and highly evocative about them.

Piping was at its peak in pre-Famine Ireland. After the Famine, the old dances began to give way to the sets and half-sets based on the quadrilles and the pipes were replaced by the melodeon and the concertina. As the end of the nineteenth century approached it seemed that the Irish pipes were fated to follow the Irish harp into oblivion. Fortunately, the national revival came about and when the Gaelic League was founded in 1893, many aspects of native Irish culture were promoted. Over the years, pipers' clubs were founded in Cork and Dublin and although they disbanded eventually, it wasn't before the tradition was passed on to a whole new generation. Na Píobairí Uilleann Teoranta (founded in 1968) has its headquarters in Henrietta Street, Dublin. This society possesses links with the past, strengthened by the discovery of old cylinder recordings (made in the first decade of the twentieth century) of pipers who were then old men. This organisation is responsible for co-ordinating the International Uilleann Piping Day in October in locations at home and abroad, events which range from recitals or workshops. The rediscovery of the pipes, at an international level, is borne out by the number of pipers from America and Continental Europe who visit Ireland each year to learn the instrument.

The playing of uilleann pipes is not for the faint hearted. Tradition holds that the mastery of the pipes requires seven years learning, seven years practising and seven years playing! They are among the most complex forms of bagpipes possessing a chanter (with a double reed) and a two-octave range, three single-reed drones and, in the complete version known as a full set, a trio of (regulators) all with double reeds and keys worked by the piper's forearms. The word 'uilleann' is derived from the Irish word 'uille', meaning elbow. A player's elbows are the method of inflation and not the mouth, a feature which differentiates the uilleann pipes from the great Highland bagpipes of Scotland.

The uilleann pipes and their unique 'personality' have entered into popular culture, so much so that there is an abundance of 'pipe jokes'.

> Q. How is playing an uillean pipe like throwing a javelin blindfolded?
> A. You don't have to be very good to get people's attention!

POSTCARDS FROM THE FRONT
(THE BAMFORTH SONG SERIES)

How I envy writers who can work on aeroplanes or
in hotel rooms. On the run, I can produce an article
or a book review, or even a film script but for fiction,
I must have my own desk, my own wall with my
own postcards pinned to it and my own window not
to look out of.

– John Banville

Imagine my delight when I discovered among the
miscellaneous stationery items bought at a car boot sale, a
selection of very old Bamforth postcards. The cards are
from the 'Songs Series Postcard Collection' which depicts
popular songs or hymns accompanying suitably
melancholic images of separated sweethearts.

These scenes are often full of longing, portraying a
soldier missing a loved one or equally, the loved one in
question pining at home, staring into an unfathomable
distance with sad eyes. Settings are usually of a very
homely nature in these cards. Roses and crisp net curtains
signify hearth and home while outdoor landscapes are
often of distant ships at sea or vast spaces which
emphasise the ever-widening gulf between the young
couple. The very first postcard to be printed in this 'Songs
Series' contains a verse from 'When the War is Over,
Mother Dear' written by A.J. Mills, J.P. Long and Bennett

Scott. The song was recorded in 1915 by English tenor Ernest Pike (stage name Herbert Payne).

Bamforth and Company Limited was a very well known postcard publisher. James Bamforth, the founder of the company, started his career in 1870 as a portrait photographer in Holmfirth, West Yorkshire before making lantern slides in 1883. The company, however, is probably best known for the range of saucy seaside postcards it produced right through the 1980s and which are still available today from booths along promenades all over the world.

The six cards in my possession though are nothing like those saucy seaside images and, as evidenced by the handwriting on all of them, they had actually formed part of a correspondence during the First World War. One of the things I noticed immediately was that the handwriting was the same on all of them and obviously by a woman, due to the content. Three of the six make up a complete set in themselves, containing the three verses of 'God Keep You in his Care'. All six cards are addressed to a 'Dear sweetheart'. One of the cards poignantly declares undying love and a longing for 'nice long walks again. Roll on 1922 and your homeward journey'. Because the cards are unstamped, they must have been included with a package or letter from home.

Bamforth & Co Ltd also started making silent films in 1989, a side of the business that lasted only a few years. By 1905, it even had a branch in the United States. The reverse of the cards reads Holmfirth (England) and New York together with its distinctive art nouveau logo. The images on the cards I found in that old cardboard box vividly evoke a sense of longing and alienation. They speak volumes for the heartbreak of separation which the war brought. As mini narratives, the cards seem 'to say it all'. One of the cards, bearing the headline, 'Love So True', shows a beautiful young girl in a heart-shaped frame looking pensive and crestfallen. In the centre of the card a soldier looks out from over a wooden fence, symbolising how war has imprisoned him. The verse on the card 'Dream-Time and You' contains the lines: 'When the gold sunset tinges the blue,/ All that I sigh for is dream-time and you'.

Another card contains a verse from 'Though the Wide Seas Roll Between Us' and shows a woman with a far away look on her face as she sits before a portrait of her beloved. In the background, the image of a ship in full sail eloquently portrays the heartbreak of a ship of dreams seeming to sail away from the harbour.

How these cards kept love alive is clearly evident. They spoke of enduring loyalty and steadfastness. On one of the cards containing a verse from 'Though the Wide Seas Roll Between Us', is written in beautiful handwriting; 'This Sunday it's a quarter past three and you have not turned up yet. We shall have tea soon so don't be late sweetheart'. Messages such as this one must have offered the consolation to men in the throes of war that simple domestic pleasures were available to them in the immediate future. It can only be imagined how these miniature postcards laden with images of ever constant devotion surrounded by fresh flowers must have had on soldiers faced with the absolute horrors of the trenches. Another card bears a printed extract from the verse 'Home Again'; 'Do you think of us sometimes, in those far-off lands,/See in dreams the eyes you loved, clasp the distant hands?' This particular card shows a soldier dreaming of his wife and family. The message handwritten on this card says: 'How sad and lonely this poor chap looks, does he not? Darling, I hope you are not feeling so sad'. Alas, some soldiers never came home from the war but I'd like to think the Bamforth Cards in my possession were returned to the sender by the recipient.

The Bayno:
A History of the Iveagh Trust Play-Centre

Rather than being a human, be a humanitarian.
– Kowtham Kumar K

Supported by Fás, this publication marks the centenary of the founding of the Bayno in the Liberties, a play-school for children which owed its existence to the benevolence of Edward Lord Cecil Guinness, heir to the Guinness fortune. Because it provided buns and cocoa, the Bayno's name grew out of the word bean-feast which was well known from the eighteenth century onwards in England and elsewhere to describe a party. It first opened its doors in Myra Hall, Francis Street in 1909, continuing there until its relocation to Bull Alley in 1915. Black and white photographs depict powerfully-evocative scenes from the Bull Alley of the 1800s, the visit of King George V and Queen Mary to Myra Hall in 1911, maypole dancing in the yard of the Bayno in 1953, together with children knitting, weaving and at play.

An opening dedication honours the memory of Martin Lacey. Before his passing, Lacey had begun the task of drafting the opening chapters (establishing vital historical backdrop to the Liberties prior to and after the setting up of the Bayno – this work is ably and substantially revised by editor Liam O'Meara). What follows is a colourful introduction by Councillor John Gallagher who, for his commitment to the Liberties, is well known in the area as the Knight of the Coombe. Gallagher's contribution is a historical gem in itself and it alone is worth the publication price. Memoir style, he recounts the social, cultural and economic conditions prevailing in the 1940s. Born in the Coombe, he attended the Bayno as a child, remembering the buns and the shell cocoa ('which was poisonous'), the camaraderie, the football and 'all sorts of arts and crafts for boys and girls'. An important point is made regarding the boys who went to the Bayno, who 'wouldn't have any ambitions of getting clerical jobs, most of them having left school early and learning to use their hands at arts and crafts was great'.

He also tells of the poverty that existed then (living in the Liberties around the Coombe at that time 'was the lowest place to live') yet, surprisingly, tells of 'distinctions between tenements and between residents in tenements'. This hierarchy of class distinction separated men and their families who had jobs from those who hadn't. Jobs in factories like Jacob's were deemed to be worth having but most got jobs in cleaning or 'in a terrible sewing factory' and for men it was mostly manual work, construction work, where 'you had to use the pick and shovel'. Sanitation was also poor. Gallagher describes children coming to school with dirty heads. He writes of those times with the authentic truth of his own first-hand experiences. A colourful illustration is as follows:

> The extraordinary thing about the tenements was that you'd hear Operatics coming out. And the great thing here on a Sunday morning was a woman who lived in number 8 on the Coombe and on a Saturday night she might take a drop too many, but on a Sunday morning, no matter how late she was up drinking the previous night, she'd start singing and she'd sing for maybe two hours. And everyone would listen to her beautiful voice.

The consuming of alcohol and the imbibing of alcohol beverages was a regular and common occurrence. The public house was like 'a little club' and also a place to go seeking information about jobs. However 'the husbands would drink more than they should and there was a lot of drunkenness'. Mainly because it was an escape from the problem of going back to the tenements 'the cold, nagging wife and a lot of children around, crying'.

The Bayno (presented in American A4 format) sets out to document how the Bayno play-school (open for three hours every day after a school day which ended at four o'clock) came about, the purpose it served and its importance in the area. Above all, it delivers a valuable insight into the grim conditions of children at that time. As early as 1729 Jonathan Swift, Dean of St Patrick's Cathedral, had satirized, in works such as *A Modest Proposal*, the treatment of the Catholic Irish and children by a Protestant monarchy and nouveau riche aristocracy. The Bayno play-school owed its existence to a philanthropic sensibility (Lord Iveagh gave £38,000 to set it up), and was 'the biggest investment in children made by a private philanthropist'. It provided heat, sustenance and learning through play right through until its eventual closure in 1975 – due to the peaking of emigration and a population decline in the Liberties. It was at its most active during the two world wars mainly because the absence of men placed more onerous burdens on the shoulders of the women.

The publication ends as it begins, on personal narrative in the same mould as that of John Gallagher. These nostalgia-free stories are by people who have their origins in the Liberties, people such as Eileen Reid and Máirín Johnston.

THE ABSENT ARCHITECT
THREE NEW ARTWORKS BY CLEARY+CONNOLLY AT THE CASINO AT MARINO

A real building is one on which the eye can light and stay lit.

– Ezra Pound

Situated at Cherrymount Crescent, just off the Malahide Road, Dublin, this Palladian-style building delivers a striking optical illusion. The top floor windows are dissimulated by the attic balustrade and the actual door is only half the size it appears to be. The two main windows are partially 'mock' to maintain the regularity of the features on the four facades which turn out to be different. Designed by eminent architect Sir William Chambers, it closely resembles a Greek temple. Chambers is the architect also credited with designing Charlemont House, Lucan House, parts of Rathfarnham Castle and Trinity College. A point of historical fascination about him is that he never came to Ireland. Instead, he trusted the execution of his work to the clarity and precision of his drawings.

On first observation, the Casino (meaning small house by the sea) appears to contain only one room. However, sixteen rooms situated over three floors offer surprise and delight to the visitor. Features include a china closet boudoir and zodiac signs in the ceiling of the bijou library. A strong cosmic symbolism runs through the building with carvings of Apollo, the Sun God and also, what sometimes has been read as Masonic symbols on the parquet floor. Thanks to the management of the Office of Public Works, the Casino, Marino is open to the public from March onwards. However, there's now an additional reason to visit this architectural gem. Having trained as architects themselves, Paris-based artists Anne Cleary and Denis Connolly, devised and put on show at the Casino, three new interactive artworks under the title 'The Absent Architect'. The artworks are mostly inspired by the obsessive dedication to symmetry offered by the building. 'The Absent Architect' was officially opened by Brian Hayes TD, Minister of State at the Department of Public Expenditure and Reform with Special Responsibility for the Office of Public Works. Oliver Dowling, Visual Arts Specialist was also present.

The Casino at Marino was originally designed as a pleasure house for James Caulfield, the First Earl of Charlemont. Caulfield, born on 18 August 1728, obtained the title at the age of six on the demise of his father. Receiving very little schooling as a boy, it wasn't until the services of his tutor Mr Murphy were engaged that he became an avid reader. Indeed, visitors today to the Casino library can see evidence of the vast range of books the library once possessed, tomes bearing medical, architectural and literary titles. Whenever he was in London, James Caulfield visited the literary celebrities of the day, such as Sir Joshua Reynolds, Goldsmith and Dr Johnson. In 1728 in the company of Mr Murphy, Caulfield, in keeping with the fashion of the times for travel, set out for the continent, visiting Holland, Germany and engaging in classical studies at Turin. He generally gave a good account of himself with all the various dignitaries and ruling families he came into contact with. He also became fluent in Italian.

James Caulfield was to travel extensively for several years also visiting Egypt, Greece and Spain. While in Rome in the 1750s he met Sir William Chambers where the plans were drawn up for the Casino at Marino. The resulting neoclassical garden temple is acclaimed as one of the finest eighteenth century buildings in Europe, an amazing fact considering its equally famous architect never saw it.

The vision Sir William Chambers had for the Casino, Marino ensures that it will continue to give pleasure to all who visit long into the future. It's an astonishing architectural feat for many reasons. It's composed principally of simple platonic forms and pure geometric elements: the overall form is that of a Greek cross, a construction of pure symmetry. The vases on the parapet are in fact chimneys, a trick which the architect Gandon, who studied under Chambers, repeated at the Custom House, Dublin. The corner columns resting on the podium double as downpipes for rainwater and continue down to the basement.

At present, again thanks to its commitment to encourage visitors to enjoy sites such as the Casino at Marino, the OPW (established in 1831) commissioned 'The Absent Architect' from Irish artists Anne Cleary and Denis Connolly. This award-winning duo have exhibited to worldwide acclaim. They are the only Irish artists to show work at the Pompidou Centre, Paris. Having trained as architects themselves, they have become Ireland's foremost new-media artists incorporating innovative technology to produce art that is engaging and significant. The work of Cleary+Connolly has a strong socio-political aspect both from its subject matter and its engagement with people. They coined the phrase 'Observer Participation' to describe their commitment to affirming the active role of people in art and in society. Exhibition sites to date include Farmleigh Gallery (Dublin, 2012), The Barbican (London 2010), The Pompidou Centre, Paris (2009) and Sesc Pompéra (Sao Paula, 2009).

'The Absent Architect' is a thrilling sensual and intellectual experience. Devices such as The Temporal-Symmetroscope send us back in time to visit the studio of architect Sir William Chambers (played by well-known actor/comedian Pat Shortt) as he discusses details with his client James Caulfield. The scene also includes Gandon (played by the artist Denis Connolly). The Temporal-Symmetroscope superimposes two symmetrical lines of time – our own and that of Sir William – allowing us to see ourselves set into a stream of events from the past.

While he lived (he died in 1799), James Caulfield allowed local people to stroll freely on his estate, a very unusual privilege afforded in that particular era. He insisted that his demesne remain unwalled, a regular occurrence in Italy but not common in Ireland. There remains from the time a sketch by Anne Caulfield, James's wife, which shows a beggar, dog and child visiting the estate. James married Anne (neé Hickman of Clare) in 1768, a woman who was considered a great beauty of the day. Lord Byron wrote of her 'for the head of Lady Charlemont (when I first saw her nine years ago) seemed to possess all that sculpture required for its ideal'. Again, thanks to technology and a device called The Stereo-Symmetroscope, visitors can avail of a modern version of the nineteenth century Wheatstone Stereoscope to play with outside views of the Casino. Peering through the Stereo-Symmetroscope, Lady Caulfield can be seen in a glorious yellow gown standing on the steps of the Casino. The original drawings of life on the estate which inspired the scenes, sketched by Lady Charlemont, are currently archived in the National Library of Ireland. The Stereo-Symmetroscope also draws on the relationship Lady Charlemont had with Lord Byron and we see them walking together while he reads his poetry to her. The alternating scenes between the eighteenth century and the nineteenth century symbolise the shift from enlightened conversation to romantic feelings. The third artwork, the

Iso-Symmetroscope is an optical device, reminiscent of eighteenth century constructions with prisms and mirrors. It allows us to examine and complete the stunning symmetries of the entrance hallway, where the coffered, semi-circular apse so strongly resembles the dome of the Pantheon of Rome.

As well as having Pat Shortt on board (in the role of Sir William Chambers), 'The Absent Architect' exhibition films were shot with the help of a large team including professional actors, local participants, pets, friends, artists and OPW staff. Thanks to the ongoing procurement, management and maintenance policy of the OPW, the Casino at Marino is just one of a host of heritage and cultural sites throughout the country well worth a visit. 'The Absent Architect' by Cleary+Connolly, which opened in March 2013, will run indefinitely.

JACOB'S BISCUITS:
OVER 160 YEARS OF BISCUIT MAKING

> Real generosity toward the future lies in giving all to
> the present.
>
> – Albert Camus

Earlier this year Tallaght Library held an impressive
exhibition which documented the history of Jacob's
Biscuits from its foundation in 1851 to its continuing status
as one of Ireland's most popular brands. It's fitting that
such a comprehensive display of memorabilia and text be
shown in this particular library. Tallaght will always be
closely associated with Jacob's, its factory on the Belgard
Road gave employment to the area from 1968 to when it
ceased production in 2009. Needless to say, the closure of
the factory was a tremendous blow to the community. A
report in *The Irish Times* cited the workers' disappointment
not only for the loss of employment but also the
camaraderie of the workplace. One female worker spoke
about the changes that had occurred in the history of the
Tallaght factory since she began working there. What had
previously been a man's world, with women doing the
packing and men performing higher skilled tasks, had
ended up a level playing field at the finish.

There are many landmarks in the evolution of Jacob's;
developments in terms of industrial, social and political
significance. As well as being renowned for the 1885
'invention' of the Cream Cracker, the memorable 'How do

Jacob's get the figs into the Fig Rolls' campaign of 1962 and the introduction of the first airtight packaging for biscuits in Europe; Jacob's were pioneers in workers' welfare. The factory had its own doctor, George P. Cope being the first GP and the firm also introduced dental care in 1907. Medical treatments were free, the only charge was two-pence if medicine was required. Unusually for the times, Jacob's introduced a staff dining room in 1900, also providing workers with a swimming pool, rooftop garden, recreation room, athletic ground and educational opportunities. Part of the welfare for workers included the setting up of a welfare department and the instigation of a savings scheme. A Co-Operative Guild was established around this time which provided vouchers to the workers for shops which could be paid back interest-free. These facilities were an attempt to keep workers away from the clutches of moneylenders who were very active in Dublin.

From a personal perspective and in keeping with the nation as a whole, I fondly remember the RTÉ programme 'Dear Frankie' and the gravelly voice of Frankie Byrne, Ireland's first on air agony aunt. 'Come Fly With Me' lasted for over two decades and was sponsored by Jacob's Biscuits. It included a Women's Page and the music of Frank Sinatra always featured. Listeners were invited to send in their problems which Frankie then introduced as being of interest because although they might not be 'your problem today, they might be someday'. As well as being humorous the programme was educational in a social context because Irish people were not used to opening up about themselves. However, Frankie Byrne's practical and witty response to problem solving was in the distant future when Quaker brothers William and Robert Jacob first took over their parents' bakery in Bridge Street, Waterford in 1851.

Two years later ambitions for extending the business were high on the agenda. No 3 Peter's Row was purchased from Thomas Palmer and Sons, the Dublin coach-making firm. Such was their success that soon the business encompassed the entire block bounded by Bishop Street, Peter's Row, Peter Street and Bride Street. Thirty years later, Jacob's Biscuits were securely established as an institution in the industrial and commercial life of Dublin.

However, this phenomenal success story was marked by misfortune. Robert Jacob died tragically in a drowning accident in Tramore in 1861 and in January 1880, a fire broke out in Jacob's factory, the flames of which were so intense that the fire was visible from every part of the city. Despite the best efforts of the fire brigade from Winetavern Street and William Street, the factory was substantially destroyed. In true Jacob's spirit, there was no delay in rebuilding. A store in Clarendon Street was rented for the labelling and dispatching of tins of biscuits. The change in circumstance necessitated that Carr's of Carlisle and two Scottish firms manufacture a number of lines of biscuits, using cutters sent over from Dublin. If the geography of Jacob's was extending (to the extent in 1912 Jacob's factory at Aintree, Liverpool began to cope with the growing demand for the export market) so too were the number of partners and family members joining the firm. When Robert Jacob died, William Frederick Bewley became a partner in the firm. George N. Jacob, the third son of William, became its first managing director. William's three other sons, Albert, Charles and William (junior) also entered the business.

On the political front Jacob's became one of the first large employers to lockout its workers during Dublin's great strike. By then, Jacob's biscuit factory was arguably among the best in Dublin. Along with Guinness, Jacob's offered some of the few manufacturing jobs in the city and positions were highly sought after and considered to be 'good jobs'. Jacob's management took a hard line with workers during the lockout. At the time, Jacob's chairman, George Jacob, sacked a man named Gibson for being in a pub. Gibson was involved in the ITGWU and immediately began to organise union activity. Jacob's women workers were the last large group of workers to hold fast to the principles of the lockout. Many of the women workers in Jacob's were members of the Irish Women Workers' Union (established by Delia Larkin, sister to Jim Larkin).

The outbreak of the Great War in 1914 also had several consequences. For one thing, raw materials were hard to obtain, scaling back the making of fancy biscuits. But the most significant was that by October 1918, 388 men from the Dublin factory and 262 men from the Liverpool operation enlisted. Of these, 52 were killed. The firm regularly sent cakes or tins of biscuits to its employees serving overseas. In November 1914, the Dublin factory loaned a 4-ton Leyland lorry to the Red Cross for despatch to the front in France. The Great War also had consequences for Jacob's premises at Bishop Street which extended into 1916 and the Easter Rising.

The Irish Citizen Army, led by James Connolly, decided that while England was distracted by war in Europe, it would be a good time to strike against it. Jacob's biscuit factory was seized as an easily secured fortress. Its advantageous position meant it would easily command the main routes to the city; from Portobello Barracks, Rathmines, along Camden Street and Aungier Street into the city. On Easter Monday, 24 April 1916, only a small number of Jacob's workers turned up for work, it being a bank holiday. These workers would carry out maintenance which could not otherwise be done when the machinery was in motion. These included fitters, firemen, boilermen and outside chimney sweeps. Some time between twelve noon and one o'clock, a group of 150 men, some armed, broke into the factory on the Bishop Street side, commanded by Thomas MacDonagh and including Con Colbert and Major John MacBride.

The rebels went about securing the building, erecting barricades at weak points. The biscuits and cakes found on the premises sustained the rebels until the Tuesday of Easter week when they were forced to go outside to forage. The siege lasted until 30 April when two clergymen from Church Street came to the factory on a peace mission. High hopes for victory ended in an unconditional surrender being signed by MacDonagh and others and read aloud to all the men. They were advised that they only had an hour to leave the factory, information that caused some of them to burst into tears and others to break their revolvers on the ground in rage. Caretaker Thomas Orr later said of the men in his statement that during the entire time of the occupation he never saw anyone under the influence of drink or using bad language. A footnote to the events of Easter Week emerged in 1961 during an exhibition night held by the Old Dublin Society. Two burnt biscuits were displayed. It was said they were made in Jacob's factory by some young volunteers who could not resist doing so despite being told not to touch the machinery. They were burnt to a cinder but the company name was still legible.

One of the survivors of the Jacob's occupation was John MacDonagh, brother of Thomas, who had fought under his brother in the factory, and was sentenced to life imprisonment. He had been a well-known opera singer in the United States and around the world when the call to arms came. After his release from jail, he went back to America and wrote a Broadway play, *The Irish Jew*, about the election of a Jew as Lord Mayor of Dublin. With so many Jews and Irish in New York, it was a big success. Another survivor from the Jacob's occupation was

Volunteer Michael J. Molloy, the printer of the Proclamation of the Irish Republic. He had marched from the College of Surgeons on Easter Monday under MacDonagh. He later became a compositor for many years with Independent Newspapers. In 1917, Jacob's annual report stated that production resumed in the factory after four or five day's cleaning up. About 100 bombs were left behind by the rebels in various parts of the factory. Compensation for looting was paid by the government.

When the Great War ended, full working capacity resumed in the factory in 1919 when supplies of raw material such as sugar were reported to be back to the 1915 level. The establishment of the Irish Free State in 1922 sparked the decision to split the company. The factories in Dublin and Liverpool became separate entities. Jacob's factory again featured in the drama of events in 1921 when Free State troops took it over to prevent occupation by Republicans.

Jacob's history with regard to its products has been varied. In 1926 the company began to manufacture chocolate confectionery. Sweets included Patricia Chocolates, Rich Milk and Chocolate Peppermint Creams. Easter eggs were also made. A memo from the factory floor from October 1934 states: 'Please note that it has been decided to alter the recipe of the Teddy Bar, increasing the malt by half pound in the nougat, and reducing the butter from 3lbs. to 2lbs. and adding 1lb. to the Nucoa'. Jacob's gave up the production of confectionery at the end of 1961, the same year incidentally that the Jacob's Television Awards were established. With the arrival of competition in the form of Boland's, Jacob's concentrated on its core biscuit business. The Jacob's Television Awards ran until 1993, honouring actors like Fionnuala Flanagan and Brendan Gleeson. Presenter Gay Byrne received a Jacob's Award six times.

In 1960 Jacob's began to export Cream Crackers to the United States under their own name; they had been barred until then because they had no cream in them. The Irishness of the product was stressed; in 1963, a round tin featuring sketches of Irish scenes was exported. Indeed, the Jacob's biscuit tins from those earlier times are now vintage treasures. Ever mindful of the company's image, the striking red flash logo, devised and introduced in 1958, replaced the original trumpeter which had been in use since the 1930s. In 1991, Jacob's were taken over by Groupe Danone, a state of affairs which lasted until Fruitfield acquired the Irish portion of Jacob's. Finally, in 2011, Jacob's Fruitfield was bought by Valeo Foods.

Eileen Casey's books include *Drinking the Colour Blue* (New Island), *Reading Hieroglyphics in Unexpected Places* (Fiery Arrow Press), *From Bone to Blossom*, a collaborative work with visual artist Emma Barone (AlTents Publishing, Rua Red Arts Centre) and *Snow Shoes* (Arlen House).

A recipient of a Patrick and Katherine Kavanagh Poetry Fellowship, her story 'Macaw' won the Emerging Fiction Category in the 2011 Hennessy Awards. She is a regular contributor to journals and magazines including *Ireland's Own, Senior Times, Poetry Ireland News, The Midlands Arts & Culture Magazine, Ireland of the Welcomes, InTallaght, The Irish Times* and *Writing Magazine*, UK.

A creative writing facilitator, she is a graduate of the Oscar Wilde Centre at Trinity College, Dublin, with an M.Phil in Creative Writing.